Dear ♡

This book was
David's – I'd like you
to have it.

Love,
Kathleen

Spinning Wheel's

Antiques
for Men

𝔖𝔭𝔦𝔫𝔫𝔦𝔫𝔤 𝔚𝔥𝔢𝔢𝔩'𝔰

Antiques for Men

edited by
Albert Christian Revi

CASTLE BOOKS

Copyright © 1974 Spinning Wheel Magazine, Everybodys Press, Inc.

Selections from Spinning Wheel: Copyright © 1950, 1951, 1952, 1953, 1954, 1955, 1956, 1957, 1958, 1959, 1960, 1961, 1962, 1963, 1964, 1965, 1966, 1967, 1968, 1969, 1970, 1971, 1972, 1973, by Spinning Wheel Division, Everybodys Press, Inc.

Published Under Arrangement With Ottenheimer Publishers, Inc.
Printed in the United States of America

Introduction

Some of the greatest collections of antiques the world has ever known were assembled by men. By nature, men "acquire" wealth, whether it be in land, stocks and bonds, or antiques. Compiled here are articles carefully chosen by the editors of *Spinning Wheel* to appeal to men who collect antiques.

Beginning with antique jewelry, this book goes on to such subjects as old smoking accessories, antique sporting equipment, woodcarvings, toys and banks, and a host of popular collectibles that men enjoy. Everything covered in this book is still within the means of the collector with limited funds. If he's selective, his antiques can be one of the wisest investments he'll ever make. And living with antiques can be such an enjoyable experience—a thrill he can recapture every day of his life.

Contemporary politics will be more meaningful to the man who collects political antiques; and old wine and spirit labels for decanters will enhance the pleasure of that after-dinner libation.

Albert Christian Revi, Editor
Spinning Wheel
Hanover, Penna. 17331

Table of Contents

Mid-Victorian Jewelry For The Gentleman

by ADA DARLING

Silver matchsafe.

THE Victorian gentleman wore black — black suits, overcoats, gaiters, and hats, reserving colored or white vests for formal events. He lightened this decorous choice by the use of rich and elaborate accessories.

The self-respecting head of a household carried a cane, frequently gold-headed, as he strolled to his office. Canes were usually ebony sticks; handles were straight, square crooks, round crooks, or pear heads. Those of gold, or gold plate, were handsomely engraved; pear heads were elaborately embossed. If space in the design permitted, the owner's name was engraved in it.

Men's rings were large and impressive—perhaps an initial outlined in diamonds on a black onyx stone, or a cameo of the tiger-eye variety.

Vest chains were heavy, consisting of two long chains fastened together by a ring which held a short chain with a bar at the end. This bar slipped into a buttonhole in the vest, and the long chains, watch on one end, accessories on the other, were worn across the front to a pocket on each side.

Vest chain accessories were many and varied. For the man who smoked there were gold cigar cutters. There were also gold toothpicks. The one pictured here screws into the handle and can be completely enclosed. Gold pencils and silver pens were often used. Charms hung from a short chain were popular. Sometimes the charm indicated the profession or avocation of its wearer — a horseman might choose a stirrup; a seaman, a "reliable compass." Fraternal emblems were in demand. For those who could afford them, there were large lockets of gold or platinum, finely engraved, flashing with diamonds. No one can deny that the man of the 1860s and 1870s did not put up an impressive front!

Silver match boxes made convenient pocket pieces. There were also tobacco boxes, quite similar to the match box

Open face, engraved gold watch.

Moss agate cuff buttons, Ascot tie pin.

Gold toothpick, shown open.

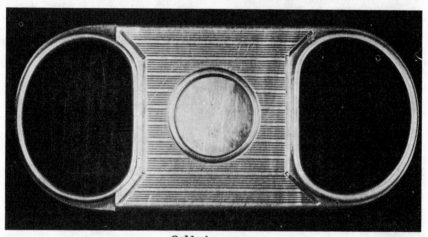

Gold cigar cutter.

pictured, but a little larger, and opening from the side.

Necessary collar buttons, shirt studs, and cuff buttons became important. Some buttons had solid posts; others separated by pressing on the little buttons on each side. The moss agate cuff buttons shown here are of the latter type. Studs in solid gold or plate, or of diamonds, vied in importance with the watch chain. A close second was the tie pin. The conventional gentleman might select a large but simple Ascot pin like the one pictured; his sportier fellows liked a tie pin as flashing as their studs. All kinds of designs were used--stars, crescents, birds, and wishbones--all jeweled.

Watches for men were thick and heavy, and flippantly called "turnips." Here the engraver did his finest work. Landscape, floral, and conventional designs were equally popular. Many cases were contemporarily listed as "18-K or plump quality."

The American Pocket Watch

by JAMES W. NEILSON

ANCIENT artifacts witness to a preoccupation with time and its measurement, and no doubt the invention of the mechanical clock, late in the middle ages, worked a veritable revolution in timekeeping. Only slightly less momentous was the development of the watch in the sixteenth century, not long after Peter Henlein of Nurnberg developed the spring-driven timepiece. Jewelry and timekeeping were now inexorably fused, presumably for all time.

The first watches were inaccurate by any standards, but improvements came steadily from the fertile minds of the later Renaissance. The hairspring dates to the latter half of the seventeenth century, and shortly after the eighteenth dawned, watchmakers began to use jewels in their movements. By the time our Founding Fathers reached the New World, watches were common among the well-to-do, though not within economic reach of common men.

Mass production of a variety of durable goods blurred class lines in the twentieth century by providing the people with goods once the exclusive property of the wealthy.

Democratization of the pocket watch, in the nineteenth century, came about through Aaron Lufkin Dennison. Before this time, importers supplied the American market with Swiss or English watches, expensive, handmade items all. The success of the New England clock industry failed to extend to the manufacture of watches, and it seems doubtful if American watchmakers turned out more than a few thousand before the middle of the century.

Pioneer Producer

Dennison was born in Freeport, Maine, in 1812, the son of a cobbler. As a boy he showed strong interest in things mechanical, utterly none in his father's trade. Seeing this, the senior Dennison apprenticed him to a Brunswick watchmaker. Some three years later, the 21-year old Aaron found employment in Boston as a full-fledged journeyman in his craft, and after a time he established his own shop.

Author's grandfather's keywind "turnip"; Elgin National Watch Co.; silver case by Keystone Watch Case Co.; thick heavy crystal typical of 1875.

Waltham watch in Dueber gold filled case; round dial, round stem, Roman numerals on face, and relatively large size, place this about 1890.

Hamilton railroad watch, movement #524609; Philadelphia Watch Co. case; purchased in 1907 by author's father, an engineer, who used it 36 years.

Dennison failed to find contentment in repairing watches made by others. He was appalled at the quality of some of the workmanship he encountered, and he pondered the waste in producing each watch by hand.

The operation of the Springfield Armory fascinated and intrigued him; he visited it frequently, noting the efficiency of producing standardized muskets by mass production techniques. Eventually his mind encompassed a scheme by which watches could be mass-produced with standard parts fabricated by machinery. That the machine tool industry of his day was incapable of producing instruments of the precision required seems not to have occurred to him. Once he did grasp that somber fact, he began perfecting the necessary machinery.

With financial backing from Bostonian Samuel Curtis, and gifted watchmaker Edward Howard, Dennison founded the American Horologue Company, and established it in a plant at Roxbury. The sponsors soon changed the pompous-sounding name to Boston Watch Company; and determined on expanding operations to a point where mechanized mass production could be more fully utilized. Much of the machinery had proven inadequate, and Dennison set about

to improve it. At last a new plant was ready at Waltham.

Success eluded Dennison. The market seemed unable to absorb the plant's output, perhaps because Dennison knew more about creating mass production than about stimulating mass demand. He was more mechanic and inventor than salesman. His company failed in the black year of 1857.

Purchased by New York interests, it became the American Watch Company in 1859, and later the Waltham Watch Company. Dennison remained as the company's superintendent until 1861. Eventually he moved to England and became an apparently successful manufacturer of watch cases in Birmingham. He died in 1895.

From such shaky beginnings, the American watch industry developed rapidly along lines which were intensely competitive. By 1870 there were at least 37 companies devoted exclusively to watch production, while some 60 firms engaged in their manufacture. Operations tended to be small scale—the 37 firms of 1870 employed only about 1800 men. The industry was marked by new incorporations, bankruptcies, and re-organizations.

Major Manufacturers

Gradually certain firms separated

Size 16 Waltham watch in a Dueber Special case; flattened bail, almost triangular stem, small size, and Arabic numbers on face date it ca. 1910.

An Illinois watch in a Keystone case of solid 10k gold; elaborately engraved; size and characteristics place it in the 1890 period.

themselves from the field of competition and gained a modicum of reputation and status. The pioneer producer which eventually became the Waltham Watch Company, was one.

Another was the producer generally referred to as "Elgin," the result of a union of three diversely talented men: John C. Adams, a watchmaker, Benjamin W. Raymond, a former Chicago mayor and businessman, and George B. Adams, a successful jeweler of Elgin, Illinois. The three joined forces in 1864 to organize the National Watch Company. It began to produce timepieces three years later, and in 1874 became the Elgin National Watch Company. It was, perhaps, the best managed of the watch companies; certainly it could boast it paid dividends from the beginning, and in its first six years had produced and sold 42,000 watches!

The Illinois Springfield Watch Company, organized in 1869, was the second producer of pocket watches in the Prairie State. After doubtful manoeuverings and two or three reorganizations, it became the Illinois Watch Company, and for years maintained the status of a major producer whose watches enjoyed high repute.

The Dueber-Hampden interests constituted another major producer. John C. Dueber founded a watch case business in Cincinnati in 1864, and in a few years his company held leading position in the industry. In 1886, it consolidated with the Hampden Watch Company, a Massachusetts concern organized in 1877, and the business was moved to Canton, Ohio.

A late birth characterized the final giant of the industry. This was the Hamilton Watch Company which came into existence in 1892 in Lancaster, Pennsylvania, primarily to manufacture railroad watches. Within a short time, its name was symbolic of extreme timepiece accuracy.

Watches For Everyone

While the major watch companies developed, competed, and produced high quality timekeepers, other firms tried to exploit a mass market. Despite generally declining prices, watches remained relatively expensive in an era when a dollar was a fair day's wage. The Waterbury Watch Company, organized in 1880, began to produce inexpensive watches some ten years after its founding. Success was immediate despite mechanical inconveniences associated with the watches, best known of which was the eight or nine foot

This watch is a Hampden; case is of solid 14k gold; probably slightly older than the 1890 models shown, though not a great deal.

mainspring that seemingly took forever to wind.

Probably the sales policies of the company, more than any other factor, led to eventual failure. The Waterbury Company sold large numbers of its watches at low wholesale prices, and they were often given away by merchants as premiums, usually with the sale of men's or boys' suits. An image of cheap merchandise, of shoddy goods at all-wool prices, came to adhere to the Waterbury; its popularity declined. The company reorganized in 1898 as the New England Watch Company, but its best efforts could not avert failure in 1912.

It was Robert H. Ingersoll who made the "dollar watch" famous. Ingersoll was a Michigan farm boy who arrived in New York City in 1879. He established a mail order business, engaged in manufacturing gadgets he invented, and dealt in bicycles and parts. About 1893 he entered the watch business, selling the cheap watches that bore his name, first for $1.50, later for one dollar. He bought the bankrupt New England Watch Company in 1914 and utilized its facilities to produce dollar watches. Over-expansion during World War I turned out to be disastrous, and the Ingersoll company was forced to admit insolvency in the '20s.

By that date the American watch industry had been rationalized into a few major firms. The halcyon years of the pocket watch were over.

Watch Cases

Watch cases could be plain, engine-turned, or engraved. For those engraved there were several favorite motifs. One was the locomotive, the monster of the steam age, generally found on cheaper watches, appealing to youths for whom the locomotive held romance and fascination.

Another, often found on the better gold-filled cases, depicted the noble woodland stag; he appeared time and again in different scenes and poses, often on the cover of hunting cases. Birds were less frequently used on watches intended for men than on ladies' timepieces where they hovered over honeysuckle, touched beaks over nests, or bore streamers of ribbons. Most of all, engravers delighted in portraying romantic cottages in dreamy, bucolic settings. Italianate villas with towers, or sharply gabled Gothic cottages were depicted in country glades reminiscent of the work of the Hudson River artists.

The amount and quality of engraving on watch cases varied with price and material. A coin silver case was plain, or ornamented with a relatively simple picture. The technique of producing the gold-filled case limited the art which could be practised on it. Lines had to be broad and shallow; delicate engraving utilizing many fine lines was impossible.

It was on the solid gold case—usually a hunting case—that the engraver's true talent could be expended. Elaborate scroll designs could be executed, fine lines cut to produce effects of most delicate shading. Many were custom made—and a solid gold presentation piece could be truly a work of art.

The Watches Men Carried

Jewelers and mail order houses were quick to realize that different styles and price ranges appealed to various segments of watch-toters.

A farmer or workman liked a heavy, thick watch of coin silver, or silver plated with brass to resemble gold. He referred to it as a "turnip." In the earlier period, before 1890, it was usually wound with a key rather than by a stem, and might be either open face or closed. In general, it was severely plain or engine turned, or with a minimum of engraving. It was designed to sell at a low price and give years of service; often it kept quite accurate time.

Railroad men needed a dependable timepiece, accurate beyond the capacity of most watches, and the industry provided them "Guaranteed to pass railroad inspection." Their cases were usually gold-filled, and normally, open face. They were expensive—from $75 up, in a day when even an engineer made no more than $100 a month—and jewellers sold them on credit, so much down, so much a month.

Office workers and small business men chose watches in gold-filled cases, albeit less accurate and less costly than those carried by the railroaders. Dudes and fancy dressers preferred hunting cases on elaborate chains or fobs.

For the man of wealth, taste alone dictated the limits of elegance in a timepiece. The elder J. Pierpont Morgan is remembered to have worn a truly monumental example of the watchmaker's art, which he combined with a cable-like chain and huge bloodstone pendant.

Watches were heavy and massive not because of technological limitations, but because the market preferred them that way. Women's watches indicated very well that the industry was capable of producing small, thin watches which kept accurate time.

Watch Chains

Up to the turn of the century, most watch chains were thick and heavy. Links, either gold or gold-filled, were made in a variety of designs from relatively simple to wondrously complex. Engraved gold fittings capped either end of the chain, and some sort of pendant was suspended from the chain proper, depending from a point near the crossbar which fitted through a vest buttonhole. For key wind watches, the pendant was likely the key itself. Legend has it that college sports first had watch keys made bearing the Greek letters of their fraternal brotherhoods.

For stem wind watches, only imagination limited what could be attached to a chain. Greek letter keys and emblems of fraternal organizations and lodges were popular. So were lockets, in a variety of shapes, engraved with the owner's initials, small compasses, plain or fancy charms from small gold amulets to carved cameos, large semi-precious stones, or of diamond-studded gold.

The dude who demanded something stunning to set off his fancy waistcoat often settled on a multi-strand chain woven from a lock of his sweetheart's hair. Properly adorned with gold or silver fittings, this "vest-guard" type of chain was high style. Other snappy dressers favored fobs rather than chains. These might be as much as six inches long, and an inch and a half wide, of gold, or spangled with semi-precious stones.

Restraint in Style

But "good taste" worked a revolution in watch accessories, too. Charms became less heavy and ornate, less likely to draw attention to themselves. Some men forgot, after the turn of the century, to wear pendants at all, though occasionally a gold-plated cigar clipper was hung inconspicuously from a narrow chain.

Rather light woven chain and small charm set with diamonds (probably simulated); average, typical chain and charm c. 1900.

Chains now stretched entirely across a vest from pocket to pocket, and bore a small penknife at one end.

Even the fob grew genteel. It shrunk to perhaps four inches in length and three-quarters of an inch in width; it was now plain gold or of cloth, entirely unobstrusive. The whole vest front display bespoke culture and gentility. The vigorous self-assertion of the 19th century was passe. Some men even left their vests entirely unadorned, and carried their watches in small pockets in their trousers, usually on plain cloth fobs.

Watch-carrying habits of the American male were changed by World War I, when the wrist watch became increasingly popular. The young men of the '20s adopted the wrist watch as their own, and by the time of the second World War, the wrist watch had triumphed almost completely. Only a few antiquarians and men of the railroad fraternity continue to carry pocket watches now. Even the railroads, one by one, are permitting their operating employees to use wrist watches. With the pocket watch,

About the Author

James W. Neilson, Professor of History at Mayville State College, Mayville, North Dakota, not only collects pocket watches and the chains, charms, and fobs that went with them, but wears them, too. A professor, he claims, has license to be a bit different. Now that his collection contains representative examples of each type of mass-produced men's watches, he looks for unusual specimens. He's seeking particularly an octagonal-cased watch, advertised in either a Sears', or Ward's catalogue of 1889. All watches and accessories pictured here, are from his collection, and were photographed

by Jerry Tastad.

something of the picturesque passes from the American scene.

The American Fowling Piece

by HENRY J. KAUFFMAN

THE current disparity between the American fowling piece's high quality and its low reputation among collectors is difficult to understand. Amidst the rush for cherry-seeders and apple-parers this object of quality and importance has been badly neglected, and very few collectors own a single specimen. There is no rush to the "auction block" when the sale of one is announced, and gun dealers say that it is almost impossible to sell one.

Although the name of the gun indicates its function, a description from the "Encyclopedia or, a Dictionary of Arts, and Sciences," Thomas Dobson, Philadelphia 1793, focuses attention on some of its unique features:

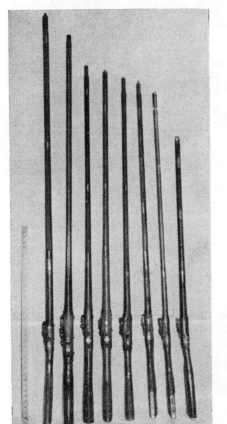

Yardstick standing beside fowling pieces indicates varying heights. All but one have curly maple stocks, most are unsigned, and barrels are octagon to round.

"Fowling Piece, a light gun for shooting birds. That piece is always reckoned best which has the longest barrel, from 5½ to 6 feet long, with a moderate bore; suitable to the game he designs to kill. The barrel should always be polished smooth within, and the bore of an equal bigness from one end to the other; which may be proved by putting in a piece of pasteboard, cut of the exact roundness of the top, for if this goes down without stops or slipping you may conclude the bore good. The bridgepan must be somewhat above the touch-hole, and ought to have a notch to let down a little powder; this will prevent the piece from recoiling, which it would otherwise be apt to do. As to the locks, choose such as are well filed with true work, whose springs must be neither too strong or weak. The hammer ought to be well hardened and pliable to go down to the pan with a quick motion."

The fact that fowling pieces should have barrels "from 5½ to 6 feet long" is doubtless the most interesting part of the description. However, it is the considered judgment of experts that very few barrels of such length were manufactured in America. It is probable, of course, that the over-all length of a fowling piece was 5½ to 6 feet, but in such a gun the barrels would have been approximately 4½ to 5 feet long. In the writer's collection of fowling pieces, barrel lengths of 42, 43, 45, 46, 48, 49, 55, 56 and 64 inches occur. Most of these barrels are of the octagon-to-round pattern, a few are entirely round, but none is entirely octagonal.

Today the long barrel myth is explained as an advantage in a business deal and not one in shooting. It is reported that fur traders swapped guns for piles of furs, the higher the gun the higher the pile of furs. Such unscientific reasoning would lead one to think that there probably were some very sound reasons for a long barrel in the eighteenth century. A contemporary account of the subject, "An Essay on Shooting," London 1789, comments on the length of barrels:

"The generally received opinion upon

Flintlock fowling piece of the late 18th century, typical of the New England simple, functional gun; style of stock is noticably different from Penna. guns; wood is a fine piece of curly maple. Barrel length 36 inches.

Fowling piece made by Isaac Haines of Lampeter Square, Lancaster County, Penna. Shows unusual side plate, carving typical of the period. The fine curl is uniform throughout the length of the stock. Barrel length 56 inches. Courtesy Dr. T. D. Duane

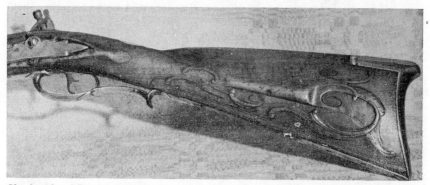

Cheek side of Penna. fowling piece made by George Eyster. Gun is not marked, but is identified by comparison with signed specimens. Eyster was one of the finest carvers of the 18th century. Stock is plain maple; barrel length 46 inches.

Cheek side of a fowling piece by A. Ernst, York County, Penna. Carving is simple but expertly executed; engraving on the side plate is unusual in style and quantity. 45 inch barrel.

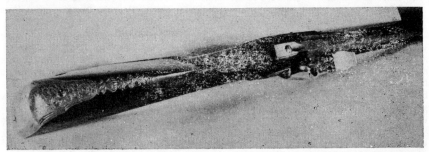

Top view of fine fowling piece once in the collection of Crown Prince Rupprecht of Bavaria. Repousse work is typical of such arms and some evidence of the European ancestry of American fowling pieces is indicated.

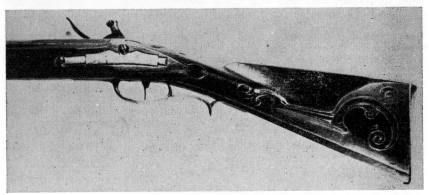

Walnut stocked fowling piece by I. P. Beck of Dauphin County, Penna. Beck, a fine gunsmith produced many rifles as well as fowling pieces. Courtesy Samuel E. Dyke

the subject is, that to obtain an increase in the range, the barrel must not only be made longer than usual, but the length and the diameter of the bore ought to bear a certain proportion to each other, and the charge of powder suited to this proportion. Because it is said, when the barrel is too short, the ball or shot quits it before it has received the whole impulse of the powder; and on the other hand, when the barrel is too long, the powder is not only inflamed, but even partly consumed before the ball or shot arrives at the mouth of the piece."

This was a time of much experimentation and the same source tells of the following interesting experiments:

"From these trials frequently repeated, we found that shot pierces an equal number of sheets, whether it was fired from a barrel of 28, 30, 32, 34, 36, 38, or 40 inches in length. Nay more, we have compared two barrels of the same caliber, but one of them 33 and the other .66 inches long, by repeatedly firing them in the same manner as the others, at different distances from 45 to 100 paces, the results have always been the same, i.e. the barrels of 33 inches drove its shot through as many sheets of paper as that of the 66 did. The conclusion from all this, is, that the difference of ten inches in the length of the barrel, which seems more than is ever insisted upon by sportsmen, produces no sensible difference in the range of the piece; and therefore, that every one may please himself in the length of his barrel, without either detriment or advantage to the range."

Arguments about the desirability of very long barrels on fowling pieces continued for many years; but by the middle of the nineteenth century the barrel length for muzzle-loaders of both fowling pieces and rifles had generally settled within a thirty-six to forty-two inch range.

Although the long barrel and light weight tended to make the fowling piece a slender and graceful gun, the fact remains that it could not share the glory of the military musket nor could it compare favorably with the rifle used for hunting big game. Many of them might be described as "ordinary" guns, but fortunately, there seem to have been some small-game hunters with good taste and great wealth, for a few very fine fowling pieces are extant today.

In Pennsylvania, the g u n s m i t h seemed to lavish his care and skill on the cheek side of the fowling piece, which naturally lacked the very functional and decorative patch-box. There he carved an extravagant array of scrolls and cross-hatchings that rival the finest carving on Chippendale furniture. Similar designs were carved around the breech tang and the ramrod socket. Intricate designs in fluting were carried on the edge of the forestock along the ramrod, and other details were added to make them attractive.

Some gunsmiths inlaid a silver plate on the small of the stock where the owner could have his initials engraved; other inlays were used as escutcheons for the barrel pins; and frequently a half moon or an eight-pointed star was inlaid on the cheek side of the stock. Some of the finest guns have intricate brass wire inlays which were simply and beautifully executed, though they lack the finesse of similar work on European guns.

A number of fine fowling pieces were manufactured by gunsmiths of the Hudson Valley. They were frequently stocked in maple and were notable for their great length.

The New England gunsmiths made large quantities of fowling pieces, for the rifle was less popular there than in Pennsylvania. The stocks were usually of walnut or cherry, occasionally in curly maple. Little carving is found on these guns but some silver wire inlay was used on the cheek side or around the breech tang. The barrel was quite long and was sometimes equipped with a bayonet lug so that it could be quickly converted for the killing of men instead of birds.

As the demand for Americana increases and the supply decreases, the fowling piece will gain in stature. They are important and attractive objects which deserve a better break in the collecting fraternity than they have received so far.

Vintage Air Guns

by LES BEITZ

The depression-era price on this later model Daisy Repeater (ca. 1933) was $3.95. It was an exceptionally high quality product, equipped with a precision sight and genuine American walnut gunstock.

SOME ADVANCED GUN COLLECTORS (and this includes a good many sporting enthusiasts, too) are on the prowl these days in quest of a rather special breed of cat. They're hot after vintage air arms. In a sort of sly manner, these buffs are poking around at auctions, antique fairs, flea markets, junk and second-hand outlets, every place where offbeat Americana might possibly be lurking, hoping to locate early model air rifles or pistols. The going is rough. These gents just aren't coming off with what one might term "good pickin's."

This is a real switch from the situation a scant half-dozen years ago. Then, most fine old American BB guns and other early pneumatic-operated firearms were pretty much classed as dinky kid stuff. Little or no attention was afforded them because there were still some good Sharps, Winchesters, Spencers and similarly esteemed old weapons to be had. Air guns simply weren't in the swim. This is understandable to a degree, because the Civil War Centennial years had focused a strong beam of interest on military muskets and repeaters of that era; in consequence, a good bit of desirable material in the vintage air gun line had been bypassed — went begging. "Big Stuff" had been center stage, and held the spotlight.

Not so today. Looking at it realistically though, the emergence of vintage air arms as a keen area of collector interest is not too surprising. It was bound to happen when a realization of the lore and background of these unique little weapons is taken into account. The idea of compressed air forcing a springed plunger to send a projectile on its way has been around for a long, long time. Matter of fact, air guns had been developed and were in use as early as the 16th century!

Let's get back to the current state of affairs and zero in on some of the fascinating antique air guns that are

still knocking about and can be picked up by vigilant browsers who have something of a fix as to what these little air guns actually amount to.

Along about the turn of the century, some twenty-odd concerns were putting out air arms of sorts. One by one, most of these outfits went "bust" —chiefly on two counts. First of all, the making of a good pneumatic valve system is extremely complex, calling for exacting tolerance and a lot of manufacturing care. Few firms have ever made the grade, including established makers of cartridge model firearms. So faulty design and poor workmanship spelled *finis* to many early endeavors in the field.

Secondly, a lot of shops that got involved in this craft, even though they came up with a commendable product, were financially unstable. They hadn't

Air Rifles

Do not expect to get the same results from an Air Rifle that can be obtained from a Cartridge Rifle. They are but a toy, yet dangerous.

Daisy Air Rifle. D 840-42

Daisy "Take-Down" Repeater.

D 884—Daisy Repeater. Magazine holds 48 Air Rifle shot. Repeating attachment extremely simple. Both the magazine and shooting barrel can be easily removed.
Length, 31 in. Weight, 1 lb. 14 oz. Price, each ....**$ .90**
Price per dozen.. **10.00**

20th Century "Take-Down" Daisy.

D 886—Same as Repeater without the magazine. Shooting barrel so arranged that either Air Rifle shot or darts can be used. Can be easily taken apart and packed in small space. Length, 31 in. Weight, 1 lb. 13 oz. Price, each ....**$.70**
Price per dozen **8.00**

1,000 Shot Daisy Repeater.

D 888—1,000 shot Daisy. A magazine gun with Winchester action. Magazine holds 1,000 BB shot and loads automatically. Working parts made of steel and brass and so arranged that any one can take the gun apart and put it together. Stock of black walnut, highly polished. Shoots accurately and with great force. The most gun-like air rifle on the market. Length, 36 in.; weight, 3 lb. Net............................**$1.25**

500 Shot Daisy.

D 890—Same as 1000 Shot Daisy except that barrel is four inches shorter and the magazine holds but 500 BB shot. Weight 2 lbs. 10 oz **$1.05**

Daisy Air Rifles advertised in a 1904 Montgomery Ward catalog. Because of its "Winchester" design, Model D888 (shown above) has a special collector interest and brings up to $35 in the current market.

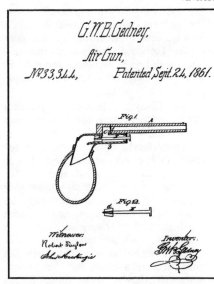

G.W.B.Gedney,

Air Gun,

Nº 33,344, *Patented Sept. 24, 1861.*

Fig.1

Fig.2.

Witnesses:
Robert Taylor
John Heating

Inventor:
G.W.B. Gedney

Left: Patent illustration for G. W. B. Gedney's air gun. Here's how it worked: Using the index finger, the shooter pushed back on the plunger to block the air passage. A projectile was then dropped into the barrel. A quick squeeze compressed the bulb-handle and the air within caused the plug to pop out. The air surged through the passage blowing out the projectile.

enough capital to merchandise their wares successfully. So, one way or another, they lost out at the marketplace.

Of these outfits, Apache, along with Plainsman and Kessler, stood their ground for awhile, then folded. Because of their limited output it can readily be reasoned that surviving specimens from these defunct firms are pretty difficult to come by. Then, too, some of these models were a nightmare of intricate mechanism in the way of operating principle, so over the years kids had buffetted them around to such an extent that they were junkers relatively early in the game. Finding one in decent shape today is really something to write home about.

The late Walter Benjamin had begun making air rifles around 1882. Because he had both a fine design and sufficient working capital, he acquired a nice toe-hold and was able to weather economic gales incident to the air gun market through several decades. Crosman and Sheridan are present-day survivors of the depression years, as well. Early examples of models put out by these firms are, of course, highly collectible. But, as mentioned, the real guns are ones that emanated from the workbenches of shops that

fell by the wayside, and a few "classics" — odd-ball types that have filtered down through the years from absolute "no name" makers. Take old Gedney's contraption, for example.

The gun that Mr. Gedney patented in 1861 is a doozie. Study the patent sketch reproduced here. If you should stumble upon one somewhere along the line, you'd do well to snatch it off the open market in a hurry because those rascals are practically extinct. They're rarer than whooping cranes. I seriously doubt if a dozen Gedneys —any condition — could be rounded up on a thorough search from Maine to California. In the lore of American air arms, they're about in the same class as a Colt Paterson, of cap-and-ball pistol fame. I'm advised that a Gedney, even in poor shape, is likely to be dickered for with an offer starting at something like fifty or sixty dollars!

The Daisy Air Rifle got its start through a rather circuituous route. In the 1880s Clarence J. Hamilton, a watch and clock repairman, teamed up with a group of businessmen in Plymouth, Mich., to produce an all-metal farm windmill he'd designed. As a sort of shirt-tail enterprise, Hamilton fiddled around with other gadgetry and eventually came up with an all-

Even at the height of the depression (1932), Webley air pistols were very expensive. Today they are in the $25 to $40 bracket.

firearm was first made available to the general public, it sold for $17. Today, one in tolerably decent condition (original and sound throughout) will bring anywhere from $150 to $200—roughly 10 times its original cost.

The Daisy "Take-Down" repeater illustrated here was supplied through Montgomery Ward in 1904 at 90¢; an *economy* model of the same sold for less than 75¢! Any one of these vintage air rifles found in good shape today will bring upwards of $25—or roughly 30 times their original price tags. So when we're inclined to growl about the high cost of living in respect to early Colts, Winchesters, and the like, it goes without saying that early BB guns are in a class by themselves. Although they're quite high priced in relation to their original cost, I honestly believe they're worth every dime being asked for them . . . and will be worth much, much more in the months and years ahead.

Why? Simply because they're fewer and farther between than most folks realize, and as the true scarcity of some of the earliest types becomes recognized prices are bound to sky-rocket.

If you play it right, you shouldn't have too much trouble ferreting out an early Daisy, Benjamin, or Quackenbush model. If you're lucky, you're mighty apt to come up with that wonderful Webley air pistol — their circa 1929 job. And if you've parted your hair *just right,* it's entirely possible you'll hit real pay dirt and bring home the fabulous 1937 model EM GEE!

So what it all shapes up to, really, is that vintage air rifles are very, very much in the swim these days.

metal air rifle which he patented in 1888. His firm, the Plymouth Iron Windmill Company, integrated the air gun into their fabricating set-up and marketed it under the name "Daisy."

As frequently happens in the topsy-turvy world of economic trends and flip-flops, the windmill end of it started to fizzle out—but the Daisy had caught on. Before long the company dropped the sagging windmill line of goods and devoted all their resources and attention to the manufacture of air rifles. The name of the concern was changed to Daisy Manufacturing Company.

Now a word or two about values— and here we get into something kind of weird. In order to establish a motif for the pattern, suppose we take a Colt .45 six-shooter, the famed and legendary "Peacemaker" of the Old West.

In early 1874 when that wonderful

Die-Stamped Powder Flasks

by EMMA STILES

Dixon flask decorated with medallions showing a dog and rising pheasant.

Brass Shell and Bush flask with carrying rings set off center; English.

Rare one-ounce Dixon pistol flask, fluted and beaded design, ca. 1858.

MASS PRODUCTION of die-stamped metal powder flasks began in the United States about 1830. These replaced flasks made of horn, ivory, tortoise-shell, mother-of-pearl, engraved brass and copper and pewter. The production of stamped metal flasks continued through the Civil War period—even after Daniel Wesson, of Smith and Wesson, patented his metal cartridge, in 1857.

Actually, powder flasks were used a lot longer than most people realize. The last patent issued for a stamped metal flask was registered by D. Wright of St. Louis, Missouri, in December 1891. At this late date most powder flasks were made of copper and/or brass, tin, zinc, German silver, and Britannia metal; rarely were they made of pewter, Sheffield plate, or sterling silver. Silver flasks were usually made to order for presentation gifts.

Die-stamped flasks can be classified into three general categories: pocket pistol flasks, military flasks, and sporting flasks. Their capacities ranged from one-ounce flasks for pocket pistols, to 24-ounce flasks for sporting guns and fowling pieces. Larger flasks were fitted with cord rings for carrying; pocket flasks were made without rings. Four

An Indian buffalo hunter and a deerhead decorate this American Arms Company flask.

Unmarked flask in a plain fluted design.

U.S. Eagle and Horn flask made by Robert Dingee, New York City, ca. 1830.

Brass flask with repousse design of dead game. American Flask Co.

Dog and Bird flask made by the American Flask Co.

Zinc Dog and Hunter flask.

Bag-shaped flask decorated with oak leaves; make by G. & J. W. Hawksley, Sheffield, England.

types of tops (pouring spouts) were made to fit the bore of a gun's muzzle or cylinder chamber—common, screw, patent, and outside patent.

Several shapes were used for die-stamped metal flasks between 1830 and 1890, but most are bottle-shaped and fitted with long or short tops. The variety of decorative motifs embossed on these flasks seems almost limitless, and collectors will undoubtedly discover many more than we are able to illustrate here. No two shapes were ever made with exactly the same decoration.

Prices were governed by the type of pouring spout, the size of the flask, and the decoration. In 1864, the American Flask Company of Waterbury, Connecticut, wholesaled flasks with common tops at $3 less per dozen than identical flasks with outside patent tops. On the other hand, one-ounce

Fluted brass flask marked G. & J. W. Hawksley, Sheffield, England.

Decorated brass flask marked "Birmingham."

Scarce copper flask marked "Dixon"; High relief design of dog and tree.

Rare Dixon (English) flask of pinkish brass with elaborate decoration.

Rare "Colt Patent" eagle flask made in England.

Brass flask with cartouches showing birds and flowers.

Handsomely decorated brass flask made by G. & J. W. Hawksley.

Elaborately shaped flask with all-over design of vines, birds, and animals.

Deer and tree decorated zinc flask; American Flask Co.

pistol flasks sold for $10 less per dozen than 16-ounce flasks. Decorated flasks sold for as much as $6.50 more per dozen than plain flasks.

Similar die-stamped flasks were produced in England and these are frequently more elaborately decorated than American-made flasks; English flasks are now quite rare.

At first, die-stamped flasks were rather plain, but as competition increased manufacturers employed artist-designers to decorate their wares to attract the trade. After 1850 decorations became more and more elaborate. Allegorical designs were very popular, and humorous subjects were frequently used.

Elegantly shaped and decorated flask. These are sometimes found with cased Colt revolvers.

Artillery Shell Art Work

by DENNIS C. MAHR

A group of artillery shell vases and trophies in various designs.

C AN an instrument of destruction be converted into an object of beauty and peaceful usefulness? Hans Lindemann, owner of the Museum of American Treasures in National City, California, says, "Yes indeed," and he has 250 pieces of evidence to back him up.

For years homesick soldiers and sailors have taken artillery shells and hand-hammered intricate designs and thoughts of home into their cold brass surfaces. They have shaped them into pitchers, cups, candlesticks, lamp bases, vases, cuspidors, umbrella stands, and gongs.

They have written names of loved ones like "Laura—1936" in a field of flowers; stamped exotic names of foreign cities and embedded coins from foreign countries in their surfaces. The most popular subject is the Statue of Liberty.

Many of the transformed artillery shells are as recent as World War II; some date back to 1809. Some are as small as 20 millimeters; others are as large as 175 millimeters. A few are quite crude, but most show a great deal of artistic talent and many weeks of work.

Almost all are easy to identify, for the month and year of manufacture, the name of the manufacturer, and the size are stamped into the base of each shell. Only in a few instances has this information been obliterated by the craftsman.

To prepare the shells for hammering, the serviceman had to fill them with lead or wood to provide a solid surface to hammer against. This padding was removed upon completion. It must have been quite a load for him to pack in his duffle bag as he moved from one combat area to another!

THE FIRST 8 INCH SHELL FIRED AT THE SPANISH FLEET ON MANILA BAY FROM THE U.S.S. NEW ORLEANS IN 1898

An umbrella stand made by the crew of the U.S.S. New Orleans in 1898 and presented to the Captain. The inscription reads: "To Spain my compliments were sent/With shell and war time ill intent/In altered shape. In friendship's name/A better fate brings higher fame."

Lindemann finds a few of his decorated shells in antiques shops; more are found at swap meets; the majority come from scrap metal yards. People clean out their garages and attics and sell the oxidized shells for scrap brass. Scrap dealers in the area save the shells for Lindemann and sell them to him at the going price for scrap brass. He polishes them up and, *voilà*, an art treasure!

Above: Pitcher and mugs made in 1944 by a U.S. Air Force flight crew; pitcher from a 105mm shell, cups from 75mm shells. **Below:** Artillery shell vases, candlesticks with Filipino coins, and a kangaroo-handled mug.

Badge first worn by Sheriff William A. Ingalls at Hawthorne, Nevada, 1894; later worn at Goldfield, Nevada. Also worn by Ingalls' son-in-law, William Mercer, from 1922 to 1935. *Collection Ron Donoho.*

Symbols of Law and Order

by PATRICK E. BOUSQUET

Badge worn by Leslie E. Snow; Snow was instrumental in the conviction and hanging of Tom Horn at Cheyenne, Wyoming, in November 1903. *Collection Ron Donoho.*

ONE OF THE peace officer's proudest possessions was his badge. He treated it with respect, and almost everyone else did, too.

Some badges were large, some were small. They were made of many different metals and in various shapes. They might be star-shaped, round with a cut-out star in the center, or of a shield or sunburst type. Usually they were of silver, nickel, copper, or brass, though gold or platinum were sometimes employed. An old badge catalog shows them in all these metals with prices ranging from $6 for the nickel to $800 for platinum examples. Occasionally a badge turns up in solid gold, set with rubies and diamonds. It was also possible to get as many as five enameled colors on a badge.

In addition to the rank of office which appeared on the badge, stamped or embossed in high relief, the officer's name was sometimes given, and some badges are dated.

Badges with a history add greatly to the interest and flavor of a collection, and most badges do have a story

behind them if the collector will research it.

A police badge from Beverly Hills, California No. 2, was given to me by Dan Thomas, the man who wore it from 1922 to 1929. Dan Thomas was appointed deputy marshal of Keeler, California, in 1918, after two other deputies had been chased out of town by some local baddies. He said the county sheriff gave him a free hand, that he played no favorites, and used his gun only when "there was no other way." After leaving Keeler, Dan worked in Beverly Hills. He died in September, 1968.

Two of the choicest badges in my collection are from Hawaii. They are not dated, but they were brought back from Hawaii in 1935. Research on these took some time to compile, but it paid off in a wealth of information.

The first police department in Hawaii was formed in 1834 under King Kamehameha III, four years after a metropolitan police force had been formed in London, England. The municipal police force was not established in New York City until 1844; it was composed of Chief of Police Kronenberg and a staff of two. The police corps organized for the Hawaiian Islands in 1843 consisted of a captain, a sergeant, a corporal, and 24 privates.

In 1845, a Marshal was appointed for the Hawaiian Islands for the supervision and control of the sheriffs of the several islands. In 1850, all soldiers

Left: Wm. J. Burns Detective Agency badge, 1950. Right: Deputy Sheriff of Los Angeles, Calif. badge, 1910-1924.

Left: Silver badge worn by a Deputy Sheriff of Kauai, Hawaii. Right: Nickel badge of the 1930 period worn by Hawaiian police.

Left: City Marshall badge of nickel is supposed to have been worn by a man named Deagan in Globe and Prescott, Arizona. Right: Nickel badge worn by a Deputy Marshall of Cheyenne, Wyoming.

Left: Nickel badge of the 1930s worn by a Deputy Marshall of El Segunde, Calif. Right: Dan Thomas' copper badge given him by the City of Beverley Hills, Calif.

on the police force were replaced by full-time police officers. By July 1861, there were 59 officers on the force. The year 1902 saw the addition of an electrical police alarm system, and in 1904 the Honolulu police station was equipped with the latest type rubber-tired police wagon.

Ron Donoho of Nevada has a fine collection of unusually interesting badges. One of his nicest is a U.S. Deputy Marshall badge worn by L. E. Snow, who was instrumental in the conviction of Tom Horn. Tom Horn was not an outlaw in the tradition of the Dalton Brothers or Jesse James, but he was undoubtedly a rough character. Born in Memphis, Scotland County, Missouri, in 1860, he left home at the age of 14 after an argument with his father. He became a stagecoach driver, guard, muleskinner, and cowhand. He worked for a while for Al Sieber, who was chief of scouts, as an interpreter—he was fluent in the Mexican language—and also with Sieber for the Army in tracking down notorious Indians.

In January 1902 in Wyoming, Horn was arrested for the murder of a 14-year old boy. Charles Ohnhaus, a court interpreter, and Leslie Snow, deputy sheriff, claimed they heard him confess to this killing. Though there was strong evidence to the contrary and it appeared that Horn was being framed, he was convicted. He was hanged November 20, 1903, at 11 a.m.

Two badges in the Donoho collection are from Hamilton and Goldfield, Nevada, now ghost towns. Hamilton, a silver mining town, came into existence in 1868, enjoyed great wealth and population, then like so many other boom-towns, had faded away by 1885. Goldfield, a late comer, was gold producing with an all-time production high of $11 million. A number of times in its colorful history, State Police were called to quell disorders. Tex Rickard's *Northern*, one of the most famous saloons in Goldfield, had a bar so long that it took 80 barkeeps to tend it.

If you elect to collect badges, the best sources of supply are other collectors, swap meets, flea markets, private individuals, and occasionally antiques shops; we say occasionally, because antiques shops are often inclined to exorbitant prices. The average price for a collector is from $3 to $15. Naturally, one of the diamond and ruby set gold badges or a platinum example will be considerably higher. Unfortunately there are a few unscrupulous people who reproduce badges, usually representing them as having belonged to famous people from old ghost towns. The beginning badge collector will do well to study existing collections of recognized collectors and listen to their words of advice.

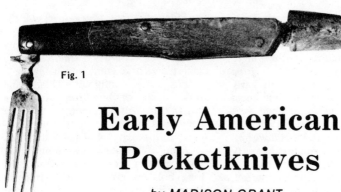

Fig. 1

Early American Pocketknives

by MADISON GRANT

SINCE THE SCARCITY of antique gun material has encouraged many gun collectors to turn to related items which are available, the pocket knife has emerged as a highly desirable collectible.

From earliest times man has utilized an instrument to supplement the dexterity of the human hand. Such devices have ranged from a single stone or club to more complicated physical arrangements, from crude bows and arrows to elaborate guns. Yet no matter how sophisticated his surroundings became, he ever remained partial to the blade, with its almost limitless possibilities as both weapon and tool. In generations past, the knife, the most universal of all mechanisms, was man's constant companion. Nor ·has modern living eliminated its fascination.

The development of the clasp, pocket, or folding knife as we know it has been centuries in the process, but its great impetus arrived with the phenomenon of mass production, about 1835. Using this date as a bench mark, let us consider the previous 75 years and the following 100 years as encompassing two distinct periods which produced knives that are still available to the collector.

The first period (1760-1835) concerns the hand constructed, highly personalized knives of the folk art type. The second period (1835-1935) deals with the mass-produced stylized

Fig. 2

Fig. 3

Fig. 4

knives commonly found today. There seems little connection between them in either esthetic or monetary value.

As a point of reference, the American Revolutionary period is a good starting place for collectors of early American knives. At that time most articles of wood, metal, or bone were made by hand and were largely the result of personal attitudes and wishes. This permitted the tremendous variety of self-expression that is the basis of collecting delight today. In this period, too, we had ceased to be a colonial appendage to England. The Continental call to arms included one of the earliest references to the subject when recruiting posters admonished each man to bring with him "his own rifle and Barlow knife."

The era of the handmade knife in the United States was relatively short. This, coupled with the Industrial Revolution, opened the floodgates of production. Demand, ingenuity, and competition soon placed a knife into the hands of every urchin, farmer, and city dweller.

Illustrated are four knives of the first period about whose origin and character there can be no doubt. Only from back country America could such pieces have come into being.

Fig. 1. A combination blade and fork, made of bog iron with horn grips, this knife is reputed to have been used by one of the Green Mountain Boys. Length, closed, 4 7/8 inches.

Fig. 2. This single spear point blade knife is from central Pennsylvania. Its long bolsters give it added strength. Horn grips with metal studs were for decoration. Length, closed, 4¾ inches.

Fig. 3. From the Valley of Virginia came this patch or hunting knife of bog iron. It has horn grips with fishtail terminal and a central fin for protection. Length, closed, 4½ inches.

Fig. 4. This single blade, with long bolsters and central panel of bone, is typical of many knives found at Revolutionary War campsites and battlefields. This almost exclusive association pretty well authenticates its attribution to the 18th century. Length, closed, 3 7/8 inches.

"Late" Pocketknives

by MADISON GRANT

Winchester knife of medium size; ca. 1930. Length closed 3''. Somewhat scarcer than the Remington, it is one of the most desirable knives for collectors.

Made by George Wostenholm, Sheffield, ca. 1880; stamped with distinct trademark, "I*XL" on handle; one of the finest, and oldest imports from Great Britain, perhaps the most popular "foreign" knife for 150 years. They are still being made. Length closed, 4¼''.

WHILE EARLY AMERICAN pocketknives are too scarce to be extensively collected, folding knives of the past century are readily available. Hundreds of manufacturers made them—in this country and abroad—and generations of men and boys carried pocketknives as a matter of course. Such knives are not bulky, have infinite variety, and are attracting more and more collector activity.

Foreign knives are generally English (no one at anytime, anywhere can quite compare with the Sheffield cutlers for craftsmanship) or German, or fall into a broad group showing Asiatic, African, or Mediterrean influence. These last tend to be gaudy, somewhat poorly made, and because they are timeless in design, difficult to date; their current value is considerably less than the others.

The source of European knives is easy to determine for the maker's name and country of origin is usually stamped on the tang of the blade, such as "Joseph Rogers and Sons, Sheffield," or "Solingen, Germany."

As a whole, the field of knife collecting has been remarkably free from misrepresentation. Recently, though, a number of foreign-made "reproductions" of high-priced American knives

of the Winchester Barlow types, have been entering this country. It behooves the collector to learn to distinguish the spurious from the genuine.

Present-day knives, due to the cost of manufacturing and assembly line methods of fitting and finishing, cannot quite equal the appearance, durability, and quality of knives made before 1935. The Great Depression of the 1930s marked the demise of most of the old-time knife-makers, and simultaneously established the cutting-off point for many collectors. In all fairness, a few present-day makers do make good products, and many collectors will carefully include the Case XX knife, for instance, with its reputation for high quality in their collections. Others feel compelled to add a modern switchblade, unlawful in some areas, which they prudently guard from falling into careless hands.

The many phases of knife collecting break down into a variety of categories, dealing with size, material, purpose, or maker's name. Some people collect nothing but pearl-handled knives; many

Bone-handled Russell Barlow knife, ca. 1880; long bolster impressed with the trademark "R" pierced by an arrow; "Russell" stamped on tang of blade. Length closed, 3⅜".

Remington knife with Boy Scout insignia, ca. 1920. Length closed, 3¼". The Remington, Russell, and Winchester represent the Big Three of American knife collecting at the present time.

prefer stag grips; others go for brass-handled types, or pruning knives. A wide field opens to the collector of pocket knives which carry advertising themes.

Pictured are four available knives of highly desirable nature. Three are American; the fourth is English, typifying the splendid workmanship from Sheffield.

Cigar Smokers' Paraphernalia

by F. M. GOSLING

WHEN THE CIGAR SMOKER of today desires a fresh cigar he selects his favorite brand at any cigar counter, removes the protective clear plastic wrapper, places one end of the cigar in his mouth, and uses his pocket lighter or a book of paper advertising matches, often given with the purchase of the cigar, to light the other end, and he is ready to puff away.

It was not always this simple. Fifty to more than 100 years ago a good bit of paraphernalia was usually called into play before the smoker could get a cigar into operation. These articles, no longer used, are now of interest to collectors.

It long has been the custom to ship cigars to the retailer in boxes containing 25 or 50. These boxes until fairly recently were made of wood,

usually cedar, and were put together with small nails. The hinged lids were nailed shut. Shown in *Fig. 1* are two styles of metal tools for prying open the lids, driving back the nails and removing them by use of the notch in the tool. These tools still can be found. They were made in a number of shapes and sizes. Some bear the name of the wholesale tobacco company.

Before manufacturers started making cigars with both ends open it was necessary to remove a bit of the sealed end in order to draw the smoke into the mouth when the other end was lighted. There were several ways of doing this. On the cigar counter usually could be found a cigar cutter. See *Fig. 2 and 3.*

Fig. 2 is made of glass with a wood

Fig. 1

Fig. 2

Fig. 3

Fig. 4

Fig. 5

Cutter at upper left bears the wording "Black & White 5¢ Cigar, National Cigar Stands," together with an outline of the nation's capitol as a trade mark. The one at top right was made in Germany. Cutter in *Fig. 5* also is designed for attaching to a watch chain. The sides are of mother-of-pearl. The top of the cigar is inserted into the end for cutting. This, also, is of German manufacture.

base. Inside are rotating knives powered by a clock-type spring. A key is attached at the back for winding. By placing the end of the cigar in the hole on top of the machine, the knife is activated, cutting the tip off the cigar. Appearing above the hole is the printed warning: "Do Not Stick Finger Into Cutter." Approximate measurements of the machine are 7 x 8¼ in. by 5 in. high. A hinged metal door in the base is provided for removal of the cigar clippings.

Fig. 3 is all metal and has two clippers. As the cigar is pressed into the hole, the clipper arm is forced down and the blade moves forward, clipping the cigar. Springs return the arm to normal position. Measurements are 10 in. wide by about 7 in. deep and 7 in. high. Clippings can be removed from the bottom. The back plate, which is attached with bolts, carries advertising for "Tirador Spanish Made Havana Cigars." The name of the maker, or of the distributor appears as "The Brunhuff Mfg. Co., Cincinnati, O."

If a counter-type cutter was not available, the smoker had other alternatives. He could bite off the end of the cigar, cut it off with a pen knife, or use a pocket-type cutter. *Fig. 4* shows four styles of these cutters. The one at lower right can be opened and used as a pocket knife, or by pressing on the back edge of the blade it passes across the hole to cut the cigar. A ring on the end makes it suitable for attaching to the end of a watch chain and carried in a vest pocket. This type, and the one at lower left can be found nickel plated, in sterling silver, and in 14-karat gold. They come plain, etched, and engraved.

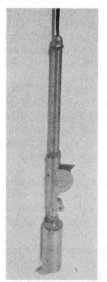

Fig. 6   Fig. 7

At the cigar counter some type of lighter usually was available. *Fig. 6* shows a battery operated one manufactured by Star Electric Co., Waterloo, Ind., and first patented in 1894. It is 14 inches long and is nickel over brass. Fuel is contained in the handle at the bottom with a wick emerging from an attached 2½ inch metal tube. The lighter was suspended over the counter by an electric cord, the other end of which was attached to a dry cell battery mechanism. When the handle was grasped and pushed back on its hinge, the wick tube moved forward; causing the end of the tube to come in contact with a metal pin creating an electrical spark which lit the wick. When the handle was released the wick tube returned to its normal position, snuffing out the flame.

A wooden box, large enough to hold the battery assembly, with the lighter mechanism mounted on top of the box is another arrangement of this type of lighter.

In cities where natural gas was available, a lamp with a gas burner often was used. Mounted on the counter the lamp burned continuously during business hours. *Fig. 7* illustrates such a lamp with one glass panel removed to show the burner. Some of the lamps used on cigar counters were quite elaborate and bring fancy prices when found today in antiques shops. *Fig. 8* shows a silverplated cigar lighter made by "The Brunhoff Manufacturing Company, Cinn., O.," makers of "Advertising Specialties" according to the markings on the base. The pierced tin shade, lined with oilpaper, reads "James G. Blaine 5¢ Cigars." The wire wicks (one is shown in front of the lighter) were heated in the flame of the oil lamp until they were glowing red hot, then they were touched to the

Fig. 9

end of the customer's cigar to light it.

Away from the cigar counter, matches were the usual means of lighting a cigar. Match safes were in common use for carrying matches in one's pocket. These are metal containers with hinged lids. They measure about 1½ inches wide by 2¾ inches high and can be found in great variety. Some are nickel over brass. This type was often produced for advertising purposes or as souvenirs of special events. Three of these are shown in *Fig. 9*. The one at the left is engraved *St. Louis* with *1904* on the reverse side and is a souvenir of the Louisiana Purchase Exposition. The middle one bears advertising for the Napa Soda Springs in California. At the right is a souvenir of the Midwinter Fair held in Golden Gate Park, San Francisco, in 1894. Depicted is the 362 ft. Electric Tower and its 8,000 lights. The reverse side shows the Administration Building.

Others were produced in 14-karat gold, sterling silver, white metal, and silverplate. They can be found plain, etched, engraved, with applied designs, polished, hammered or set with diamonds, sapphires, or other stones. Some have raised ornamentation and space for a photograph, with mica cover.

Fig. 8

Fig. 10

Fig. 11

Fig. 12

Fig. 10 shows a match safe with a cigar cutter on the bottom. The entire cutter is hinged to the match container and can be opened to remove the cigar clippings. The ribbed striking edge, usually on the bottom, appears on the lid of this combination match safe and cutter.

Small cardboard or wooden boxes of matches were sold at cigar counters for one cent a box. These often were dispensed through a machine such as shown in *Fig. 11*.

Advertising signs in the cigar category are also collectible. Although they can take up a lot of space in a collection, they are colorful and interesting. *Fig. 12* shows a metal sign in red, green, gold and brown, measuring 27 x 19 inches.

English Papier-Mache Snuffboxes

by SHIRLEY SPAULDING DE VOE

Fig. 1: Samuel Raven's painting of George IV, after a portrait by Sir Thomas Lawrence, on a large table snuffbox.

Fig. 2: Papier mache snuffbox with bucolic scene.

Fig. 3: Papier mache snuffbox with picture of a "Terrier" by Samuel Raven. Collection Mrs. Sherwood Martin.

IN THE ENGLISH CITIES of Wolverhampton and Birmingham the manufacture of japanned wares was an important industry from 1750 to 1914. Fancy articles of papier mache were produced in great abundance, from the smallest button to a piano case. But the earliest and most popular product before the introduction of the tea tray was the papier mache snuffbox.

They were produced in such large numbers and the demand for them was

Fig. 4: Underside of "Terrier" snuffbox lid reads: "S. Raven Pinxt/Favored by H. R. H. The Duke of Sussex/& Prince Leopold."

so great that they were reasonably priced and so were in reach of the majority of the people. There were small ones for the ladies and larger ones for inns, the mess hall, for family use, and to hold a gentleman's tobacco *(Figure 1)*. Pocket boxes had hinged lids and were generally rectangular in shape while the round ones with lift-off lids were for table use.

In 18th century France, papier mache boxes were made of used paper, gathered in the night by the billboard strippers, but English manufacturers were required to use paper on which full duties had been charged and which had not been used for any other purpose. An excise officer was stationed at every paper mill where he weighed, labelled, and numbered the paper bundles, a circumstance that was a hindrance and an annoyance to the paper makers for it slowed production. The government also required the manufacturers of papier mache wares to be licensed.

The early boxes were made of hand molded pulp but later a durable panel of laminated paper was used. This panel could be worked with carpenter's tools or in a drop press that punched out the blank forms.

When the gray boxes were formed they were dipped in a black tar varnish called japan, the English substitute for Oriental lacquer. The boxes were then oven dried, polished, and ready for the

decoration. The designs were executed with paint, pearl shell, gold leaf or bronze powders and depicted landscapes, allegories, *chinoiseries,* popular paintings and portraits of royalty or famous people, reduced in size to fit the lid.

In the book, *Emma, Lady Hamilton,* by M. Hardwick, 1969, we learn that Emma, saving her charms for Sir William, wrote him in 1787 to say that a portrait of herself on a snuffbox "shall not be too naked for it would not be so interesting . . . it will be seen a great deal and those beauty's that only you can see shall not be exposed to the common eyes of all and wile you can even more see the originals others may gess at them for they are sacred to all but you . . ."

Early in the 19th century engravings of heroes, special events, and bucolic scenes were available. These were made to exactly fit the lids of the flat, round boxes *(Figure 2).* These black and white prints were glued to the lids, then hand colored and varnished.

John Taylor of Birmingham (d.1775) was considered the largest manufacturer of japanned goods in the mid-18th century. His products were trinkets, gilt buttons, and papier mache snuffboxes. The latter were finished with a thumb-grained, imitation tortoise-shell and with designs in bronze powders. One of his japanners received a farthing for each snuffbox he painted. There followed many other manufacturers of papier mache

Fig. 5: Papier mache snuffbox with square of pearl shell on which the picture was painted. Author's collection.

some of whom impressed the firm's name on their products, but the work of the ornamenter can rarely be identified by name.

One who signed his boxes was Samuel Raven (1775-1847), also of Birmingham. He specialized in painting snuff and tobacco boxes. *(Figures 1, 3 & 4)* His name and sometimes the title of the subject were painted inside the lid, but between 1815 and 1831 he was pleased to add in a color called sealing wax red, "Patronised by H. R. H. the Duke of Sussex and Prince Leopold." *(Figure 4)* It is interesting that any boxes painted by his appren-

tice, to which Raven added the finishing touches, were not signed.

The habit of taking snuff was first practiced in 17th century England. M. M. Curtis in *Snuff and Snuff Boxes*, 1935, gives the surprising fact that the puritan Mistress Campbell believed in the social maxim: "She that with pure tobacco will not prime Her nose, can be no lady of the time."

The habit, apparently, had become universal prior to the first year of the reign of Queen Anne, 1702, for it is said that there were then 7000 shops in London where snuff was sold.

Queen Charlotte took snuff liber-

Fig. 6: Papier mache snuffboxes with painted scenes. Author's collection.

Fig. 7: Small papier mache snuffboxes imitating tortoise-shell. This was done by first painting the box red, then putting an irregular coating of black over the red paint. Collection Mrs. John Clarke.

ally, but her son, George IV, used his snuffbox more for show than for use. Although he went through the correct motions he never allowed the snuff to enter his nostrils. In the accounts of expenditures for his coronation, the large sum of 8295 pounds, 15 shillings and 5 pence was spent on snuffboxes for visiting foreign ministers.

Everyone carried a snuffbox and in Regency days the choice of the right box for the right occasion was important. Often they were matched to the dress, to the occasion or the time of day. There were also rules for taking snuff properly, so important that schools were formed in which correct ritual of taking snuff was taught. An advertisement in the *Spectator* for August 8, 1711, says "the exercise of the Snuff Box according to the most fashionable Airs and Notions in opposition to the Fan will be taught with the best plain or perfumed Snuff at Charles Lillis & Co."

The rather complicated ritual was as follows: "After the snuffbox was drawn from the pocket by the left hand, the fingers of the right hand gave the cover three taps, then the box was opened and a pinch of snuff placed on the back of the left hand or on the thumb nail enclosed by the forefinger and so inhaled."

At one time snuff was thought to have medicinal and curative powers and Scotch snuff in particular was considered to be an infallible means of destroying crickets. Mr. Payne, located at the Angel and Crown in St. Paul's churchyard, offered his snuff at 3 shillings, 6 pence a bottle, as an "unparalleled Specifick Tincture . . . as an assured cure for leanness."

Just as with the lighting of a cigarette today, snuff taking was useful to fill a lull in a conversation or to cover an embarrassing moment. Also an attractive box might provide a grateful change of subject. But unlike the smoker who must have a light to enjoy his tobacco, the snuffer had no need for a tinder box, candle flame, or hot ember.

Not all so-called snuffboxes were actually used for powdered tobacco. Many were made to hold patches, "comfits," bonbons or powder. But whatever its long ago purpose, an attractive papier mache box is a suitable container for today's saccharine or vitamin pills.

Koopman "Magic Pocket Lamp," patented 1889, believed to be the first American-made fluid and flint lighter.

Early Cigarette Lighters

by SAM A. COUSLEY

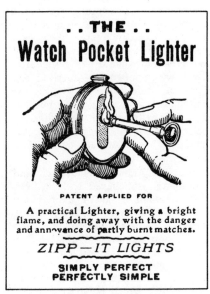

Watch pocket lighter, popular in the late 1890s and early 1900s, used synthetic flint and asbestos wick on the striker. Fuel was alcohol or naphtha.

ALTHOUGH THE 1920s focused attention upon the many handy "name brand" cigarette lighters of the fluid and flint class—Ronson's, Zippo's, Dunhill's and others—which rapidly became "must" trinkets for the feminine purse and the male pocket, the use of these little machines was not so much an innovation as a revival in modern dress of a device in use for more than 100 years.

The swank instantaneous lighter of today is actually an improved version of firemaking equipment which is older than the Roman Empire—the tinderbox. Requisites of the venerable tinderbox were a quantity of very dry, readily combustible material—tinder—and a piece of flint with which to strike sparks into the tinder by crashing the flint with a sharp glancing blow against a piece of tempered steel. For the steel an old file, a piece of sword, or knife blade would suffice. The tinderbox itself was merely a tight, dry container for the tinder, flint, and steel. It could be of most any material—wood, horn, metal, sometimes leather. It usually was kept in the kitchen or any other place convenient for starting the household fires.

The first pocket lighter was simply a pocket tinderbox, the need for which was recognized immediately after the tobacco smoking novelty was transported from the Americas to Europe in the 16th century. It was soon found that a most reliable kind of tinder for portable firemakers was a loosely-woven soft cotton rope, called "match," which was used to fire the "matchlock" muskets of the 15th century.

This "match," which was impregnated with saltpeter (potassium nitrate) would, when lighted by a spark, burn slowly with a glowing ember without bursting into flame. Some of the first smokers' pocket lighters, called "tinder tubes," used this type of fuel. Progress eventually replaced the striking steel and fragment of flint with a knurled wheel attached to the match tube which could be revolved against a particle of synthetic flint—a composition of cerium and iron filings—to obtain the spark. However, small pocket tinderboxes, complete with tinder, flint, and striker, continued to be used in this country until long after the Civil War.

In the 17th century mechanics adapted the firing mechanism of flintlock guns to create a pistol-like pocket piece which ignited tinder, instead of gun powder, when fired. Soon after Japan was opened to American and European trade in the 1850s, Japanese craftsmen began making tiny but precise adaptations of the flintlock mechanism for small egg-shape pocket lighters. These were among the first Japanese exports.

The first American-made fluid and flint lighter is believed to have been the Koopman Magic Pocket Lamp patented in 1889. It was an automatic instantaneous firemaker. When a knob on the side was pressed, the lid flew back and a spark ignited a wick. The fuel was alcohol. Spots of a synthetic flint composition were spaced around a paper disk which revolved against a sharp steel point to strike the spark. A packet of replaceable disks was provided with each pocket lamp sold.

Several lighters in the shape of pocket watches came out in the 1890s, and in 1907 there was patented the most interesting and ingenious lighter of all time. Working on the principle of catalysis, the lighter has a cylindrical wick wet with high grade alcohol. When a particle of sponge platinum (the catalyst) is introduced into the chamber containing the wick, the thin film of pure oxygen which always surrounds platinum combines with the alcohol vapor to produce a flame which lights the wick.

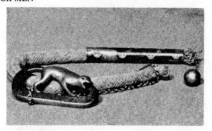

Brass (silver inlaid) tinder tube, using match tinder, has a brass monkey with tempered steel tail for a striker; piece of flint is carried separately. Silver ball attached to match extinguishes ember when pulled against the tube.

This type of lighter, which is still being manufactured and sold by the New Method Co., Bradford, Pa., is based upon the Dobereiner Lamp, invented by Prof. Johan W. Dobereiner, Jena University, Germany, in 1823. The Dobereiner device generated hydrogen by means of zinc and diluted sulphuric acid, and when a stream of hydrogen issuing from a fine nozzle played upon a small piece of sponge platinum, the platinum became incandescent and the hydrogen ignited. The principle was used to some extent in the gaslight era to provide a simple automatic instantaneous method of lighting ordinary gas jets.

During the last 50 years, pocket and table lighters have been produced in hundreds of fascinating shapes. Long ago people started making collections of them. Some collections are quite impressive. For instance, Anthony Donofrio has more than 200 fantastic examples on display in his Hackensack, N.J., barbershop—a wonder and pleasure to his patrons.

OTHER COLLECTIBLE CIGARETANA

Cigarette smoking is generally believed to have been introduced to this country in the last half of the 19th century by southern Europeans who settled in New York. Until the early 1880s, the custom was mostly confined to the New York metropolitan area.

Since the 17th century, "papaletes" (paper wrapped tobacco tubes) were the poor man's cigarette in Spain.

However, there was a distinctly American cigarette popular in the Southwest from before the Mexican War. This was a roll-your-own corn shuck cigarette smoked by women as well as men, according to reports of early travelers over the old Santa Fe Trail. Spanish-speaking natives of the then Mexican territory carried the "makings" in the pockets of their fancy vests so that smokes could be rolled as desired, and in their pantaloon pockets there was always a flint

Ormolu and agate purse tinderbox which once belonged to Susan B. Anthony. Top has alternating white and red agate slabs. Ca. 1840. Length 2 5/8".

Lighter which uses match cord tinder (lower end protrudes from bottom of case). A turn of the ring on side revolves small wheel of synthetic flint composition (cerium and steel filings) against a fixed steel striker. Resulting sparks fall on charred end of match tinder to ignite it. Illustration three-fourths actual size.

and steel and a roll of cotton tinder for producing the needed light.

If, as it seems possible, the present decline in cigarette smoking continues, there will likely be a corresponding interest on the part of collectors and antiques buffs in the accouterments thereof. More people than ever will be

searching out "cigaretana" and here are some of the items they'll be looking for:

Cigarette Cards bearing pictures of stage folk, ball players, prize fighters, ships, birds, and animals, going back to such popular Gay '90s smokes as Sweet Caporels, Admirals, Dukes, Cameos, Conquerors, and Judges, and the colorful card albums published by some manufacturers.

Miniature rugs and blankets of cotton flannel and small colored silks, bearing pictures of presidents, zodiac signs, college emblems, emblems, various national flags and state seals; some of these woven on Jacquard looms like Stevengraphs, distributed with cigarettes in the late 1890s and early 1900s.

Cigarette boxes, the colorful cardboard type which held Turkish Trophies, Hassans, Helmars, and Egytian Deities of the early 1900s; Melachrinos, Makaroffs, Moguls, English Ovals, and London Lifes of World War I years; and the 50-pack tins and the 20-pack paper wrappers of such well-known smokes of the 1920s as Omars, Fatimas, Lucky Strikes, Camels, and Chesterfields. Nor must we forget the various denominations of *revenue stamps.*

Cigarette stompers, popular in brass and aluminum animal shapes in the 1920s and 1930s. *Cigarette holders* (some with the first cigarette filters) which appeared in many varieties in the 1930s and 1940s.

Vest pocket "roll your own" devices, which utilized grain tobacco such as Bull Durham and Duke's Mixture, and Riz la Croix papers. These were widely advertised for smokers who preferred "homemades" to "tailormades," but did not "possess the manual dexterity to twist their own," even with two hands. Any Western cowboy, of course, could roll beautiful smokes with one hand while galloping his cayuse across the prairie.

Matchsafes, designed early in the 19th century to protect person and clothing from the dangerous consequences of carrying those first, completely unreliable, friction matches,

and popular till penny pocket boxes
and matchbooks reduced them to
obsolescence.

Small safety match boxes, foreign
and domestic, with their colorful
labels, and *advertising matchbooks.*

Most treasured of all cigarette
collectibles are the *pocket lighters*
which have long proved practical for
those who smoke and often convenient for those who do not.

Patented in 1907, this ingenious lighter
operates in a manner that seems magic.
Here, the silver case is shown closed but at
the right is a lid from a similar lighter. The
large cylinder is lined with a wick saturated
in high grade alcohol. Suspended from a
protective cage in the lid of the smaller
cylinder are several platinum wires on which
are strung two sponge platinum globules.
When this wire is inserted into the alcohol
gas-filled large cylinder, the platinum
instantly heats to incandescence and the
circular wick is ignited.

Sterling silver tinderbox bearing London
hallmarks. Steel attached to back edge.
Holds a small quantity of tinder, some sul-
phur dips, and tiny agate flint. Ca. 1800.

Ashtrays with Faces

by MARCIA RAY

AS A BOY, Robert Jones collected cap pistols. Later, employed by the Old Mercantile Trust Co. (now part of the Chase National Bank) in New York City, he branched out to toy banks. On retirement, his collecting interests advanced to that gaslight age symbol of affluence and prestige—the cigar. Cigar cutters and lighters of every type, tobacco containers, advertising trays and posters, and other tobacco memorabilia of the late 1880s and early 1900s fell within his province.

Among the tobacco memorabilia Mr. Jones is still collecting, are the turn-of-

the-century ashtrays cast in bronze, brass, or tin. They are as amusing and ornamental as ever, though perhaps less useful in these present days of "keep it easy to clean."

The designs on these cast ashtrays represented all facets of everyday life, from flowers and fish to farm animals and drinking scenes. Humor of a rather macabre sort was not neglected; among Mr. Jones' rarities are a skeleton, a coffin plate, and a Turkish toilet!

Rarely do these castings carry the artist's signature; almost never the name of the foundry. Only those used for advertising, bearing the name of the advertising firm and its product, can be pinpointed as to date.

An especially fascinating category of design is the "face" ashtray. A few of these from Mr. Jones' extensive collection are shown here. All are of brass with the exception of the man with eyeglasses, which is iron. None are marked in any way. They seem not to be reproductions of any known pictures, but designs born of the artist's whim and fancy to catch the smoker's eye. If some were designed for a specific club or organization, no indication of such appears.

Railroadiana

by CLARA and WILLIAM B. NISBET, JR.

THE DISTINCTION of being the first steam locomotive to operate successfully goes to the "Rocket," brain-child of the English inventor, George Stephenson. This little engine opened the era of steam locomotion when it took to the tracks in 1825.

In the United States, an import, the "Stourbridge Lion," made the first successful rail trip in 1829. A year later, Peter Cooper constructed an experimental engine, "Tom Thumb." This diminuitive locomotive, weighing only one ton and having drivers only 2½ feet in diameter, launched the Age of Steam on this continent.

The first trials were faltering, sometimes tragic, sometimes ludicrous. For instance, the "Best Friend" ran successfully for a year, then blew up

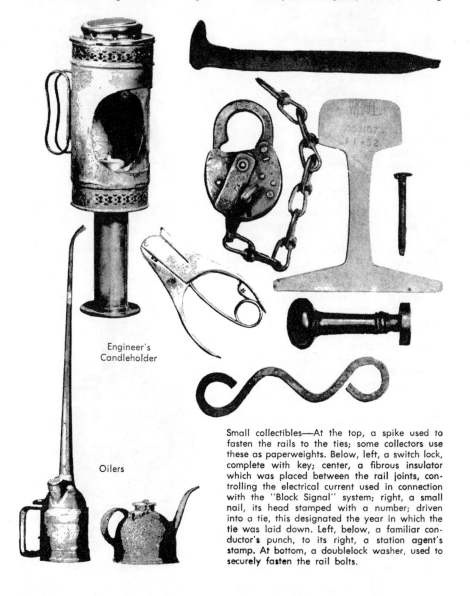

Engineer's Candleholder

Oilers

Small collectibles—At the top, a spike used to fasten the rails to the ties; some collectors use these as paperweights. Below, left, a switch lock, complete with key; center, a fibrous insulator which was placed between the rail joints, controlling the electrical current used in connection with the "Block Signal" system; right, a small nail, its head stamped with a number; driven into a tie, this designated the year in which the tie was laid down. Left, below, a familiar conductor's punch, to its right, a station agent's stamp. At bottom, a doublelock washer, used to securely fasten the rail bolts.

Engine Bell

and smoke, the flash of the driving rods, the shriek of the steam whistle which gave the steamers their impression of power and speed. In true American fashion they were recklessly exported, ruthlessly junked to railroad graveyards, there to be picked over by collectors of railroadiana who removed everything they could carry off.

The following paragraphs describe the collectibles illustrated here, and suggest others.

Builder's Plate — Shown here is a

Souvenir Knife

Flagman's Early Lantern

from no constructional fault; the fireman, irked by the sound of steam escaping from the safety valve, fastened down the lever, then sat on it. The resulting explosion injured him fatally.

In 1832, Matthias Baldwin, who was later to found the famous Baldwin Locomotive Works, introduced his version of a steam engine, "Old Ironsides." This engine, weighing 5½ tons, was so under-powered that the inventor and his two machinists were compelled to push the contraption to get it moving, then hop aboard.

From these beginning, the era of the steam engine developed with increasing brilliance for nearly a century. In the speedy "Hudsons" and the brawny "Mikadoes," the United States had superb engines, equal to anything the rest of the world had to offer.

The steam locomotive became a part of the economy of this country; it played such an important role in the winning of the West that some enthusiasts go so far as to claim that the "Diamond Stack," rather than the Covered Wagon, should be the symbol of Western expansion.

Then, for economic reason, these giants were relegated to the scrap heap in favor of the more practical diesels. In a few short years, gone were the streaming plumes of steam

plate from the Baldwin Locomotive Works of Philadelphia, Penna. It is 16 inches in diameter, slightly curved to fit the shape of the engine boiler where it was affixed.

Matthias Baldwin was the founder of this company, building his first locomotive in 1832. He was successful in the business and took as his partner, Matthew Baird in 1854. At the time of Baldwin's death in 1866, his concern had manufactured 1,500 locomotives.

Locomotive Whistle

Engine Number Plate

Engine Number Plate—This engine plate, #159, was burned in a wreck of two freights, south-bound, one foggy night in 1926, on the Berkshire Division of the New York, New Haven & Hartford Railroad. The second train, with engine #159, was operating on "Close In" orders calling for caution. Nevertheless, it was high-balling along through the fog when, rounding a curve, it came suddenly upon the preceding train which had developed a hot box and stopped, its flagman not having sufficient time to get far enough out.

The crew of #159 saw the markers on the caboose ahead, put on the air, and "joined the birds," jumping to safety. Engine #159 then ran through twenty-three cars and the caboose. The cars were loaded with apples, candy, shoes, cement, coffins, and crockery, all of which were strewn along the road bed. Incidentally, this was the last time that a "Close In" order was ever issued on the New Haven.

The practice of numbering locomotives was adopted in the latter half of the 19th century. Before that, they were named, some for famous men such as the "DeWitt Clinton," some for characters in mythology as "Mars." Still others were named for powerful or fleet animals as "Lion" or "Antelope." One busy little switch engine was dubbed "The Bee." Though engines were referred to as "she," the use of feminine names was considered bad luck; two exceptions were "Lady Washington" and "Hecate" (Queen of Hades).

Locomotive Whistles — Railroads had not been in operation long before the need arose for some warning device for crossings and track trespassers. In England, in 1833, the early locomotive "Rocket" was equipped with a "steam trumpet." It is thought that the first engine in the United States to be equipped with a whistle was the "Eureka" of the Sandusky & Ohio Railroad.

These early whistles, such as the one pictured, were single-throat affairs which emitted a high, piercing shriek. The "chime whistle" later replaced these, and its more musical note was welcome indeed.

Builder's Plate

Locomotive Headlights (from left): whale oil; kerosene, electric.

Besides their use as warning devices, whistles were used in a standard code of signals, giving information to the train's own crew as well as to crews of other trains.

Engine Bells — Early engine bells were hung in a cradle and were activated from the cab by a cord. In later models, the bell itself was stationary while the clapper was set in motion by compressed air.

Bells were used, in connection with whistles, as warning signals. Their ringing also announced the departure of the train from the station. History tells us that on the initial run of the "DeWitt Clinton," the conductor blew on a little tin horn to warn that the train was about to depart.

Engineer's Candleholder—Pictured here is an engineer's candleholder's with shutter as protection against the candle's being blown out, and a push-up arrangement for the candle. It is of brass construction with flaking green paint, which suggests that it dates back to the era of "brass and paint" when railroads vied with each other in the coloring of their locomotives.

Red stacks, vermilion wheels, with greens, blues, and yellows used on cab and tender were not uncommon. Some of the engines pulling the "varnish" (fast luxury trains) were even decorated with paintings, which included portraits and landscapes done on the sides of cab or tender. Brass was in extensive use as bands encircling the boiler and in the construction of sand boxes and wheel covers. Engines were kept scrupulously clean and polished.

Locomotive Headlights — As the early trains covered only short distances, they made daylight runs. In 1833, Horatio Allen, foreseeing the future need for night-lighting made an experiment along these lines. He arranged to have the engine push two flatcars ahead of it. The first one was loaded with sand, atop which was an iron receptacle where pitch-pine knots burned brightly, lighting the track ahead.

The Boston & Worcester is thought to have been the first railroad to equip its locomotives with headlights. These were large, square sheetmetal boxes, having a lamp and a reflector.

Shown here are three types of locomotive headlights. One is an early specimen of sheet-iron with a whale-oil lamp; the next is a type such as was used about the turn of the century, its kerosene lamp an improvement over earlier lamps; the third is a modern, electrified example. Shown together, these photos indicate comparative sizes of headlights.

Lights and Lanterns—In this field can be found quite a variety from

Souvenir Matchbox

which collectors may make a selection. There are switch lights, such as the one shown, as well as several types of flagman's and brakeman's lanterns. The brakemen used lanterns with clear glass, while the flagmen used those with green (okay, amber (caution), and red (danger) colored lenses. Classification lights, displayed on the engine to designate type of train following, whether another section or a special, have clear and green lenses. Caboose markers with one red and two green lenses designated traffic moving in the same direction. In all of these, specimens bearing the insignia of the railroad are preferable.

Crossing Sign from an abandoned division of the N.Y.N.H. & H.

All oil burning lanterns and lights were banned with the coming of the diesels because of fire hazard. Electric torches and lights are now the only kind allowed.

Conductor's Cap—In the first days of railroading, the train's procedure was governed by the engineer. The conductor's duties were limited to overseeing the disposal of freight and passengers.

In 1842, however, Capt. Ayers, a conductor on the N.Y. & Erie R.R., tiring of his inability to eject fractious passengers until a regular stop, took matters in his own hands. He ran a string the length of the train to the engine where he attached a stick. When this stick was raised by a pull on the cord, it was the signal for the engineer to stop the train. The engineer resented this intrusion on his authority; he removed the stick, and ignored the conductor's orders.

The upshot was a fist fight between the two men which ended in the engineer's defeat, and which settled the argument of authority. Thus the conductor became what his name implies: chief executive of the train and crew.

Oilers—All during the era of the steam locomotive, the engineer was seen to descend from the cab at major stops, and with the long spouted can,

Conductor's Cap

lubricate obscure but important points in the mechanism of the drivers and the rods. The smaller can held a reserve supply of oil.

Other Items—In addition to these functional items, there are those which are classed as souvenirs. One such is the little metal matchbox with railroad insignia on the cover; on the back are the names of officials of the road in raised letters which afford the scratching surface. The little knife is also in the souvenir class.

In the field of "paper," the collector can find old timetables, tickets, and passes as well as old payroll sheets and rule books, and photographs of early engines.

Paper lanterns saved from a parade for U.S. Grant in 1868. The one at the far left has a picture of Vice President Henry Wilson on the other side.

Torchlight Parades
of Long Ago

by SAM A. COUSLEY

THE PARADE LANTERNS and torches which remain as relics of the boisterous political rallies in the days of Lincoln, Grant, Greeley, Hayes, Cleveland, and McKinley are among the most exciting, romantic, and valuable mementoes of the nation's long series of quadrennial jamborees to choose a president.

The party rally, with its miles of tricolor bunting and flags, its blaring bands, bombastic oratory, clambakes, barbecues, and beer was always climaxed by a spectacular torchlight parade, awesome in its eerie dramatic appeal.

Whether in the large city or small town, a rally for any party at all drew everybody and his cousin for miles around in best bib and tucker and with lunch baskets holiday-packed. Party supporters came decked out in picture

ribbons, buttons, and scarves boosting the candidate and carried canes, horns, whistles, flags, rattles, and other impedimenta of the carnival day. Opposing party affiliates were there also—just for the excitement and fun.

Early in the morning, hitching space at the public racks around the square or along Main Street was as scarce as a parking space at one of today's Washington's birthday supermarket sales. Nags of latecomers had to nuzzle their nose bags on remote side streets.

Small boys and dogs congested, sniffing and drooling, around the spit where a steer (or at least a side of one) sizzled and dripped delicious heady juices into the basting trough. Women exchanged gossip and recipes at ice cream and lemonade stands, and voters in work shirts and blue jeans fraternized in the common cause with the boiled shirt and frock coat cadre around beer and cider kegs. Everybody was friendly and the crowd congenial, unless some beer-emboldened loudmouth of the opposing party happened to speak out of turn. That could lead to mayhem—joyous, exuberant mayhem, while the band played on!

Capital-letter feature of the day came in the evening when marching clubs from all parts of the country gathered to participate in the big torchlight procession. Mostly the clubs were made up of members of the various fire brigades, militia companies; and athletic groups. Sometimes social organizations joined the march by simply slipping into special uniforms consisting of oilcloth caps and capes, designed to protect clothing from dripping kerosene and errant sparks from the Roman candles carried in shoulder bags to explode in fancy rhythmics on signals from the leaders. Occasionally an awning caught fire and once in a while a low flying

Tan, yellow, red and black 20" diameter spherical paper candle lantern bearing wood-block designs and a picture of Grover Cleveland. Such lanterns were manufactured by Sprague & French of Norwalk, Ohio, and were common in the campaigns of the last half of the 19th century.

green or red fireball sailed into a collage of birds and flowers on some lady's hat.

Torchlight parades had their origin with the early fire-fighting organizations which used pole lanterns and torches to light their way through dark streets on a run to answer an alarm. The rollicking, adventurous "fire laddies" always were ready to make exhibition or practice runs or trot out their equipment to add zest to a parade. The first five presidents, Washington to Monroe, were elected without fanfare. For them there was scarcely any campaigning, but feverish competition characterized all of the other early elections.

Pierced lanterns with the perforations spelling the names of such candidates as John Quincy Adams, Andrew Jackson, Henry Clay, Martin Van Buren, and others, made to hang in windows or to carry in parades, have been preserved by collectors. Square candle-burning tin lanterns with their glass windows bearing wood block pictures of candidates cut from newspapers were

Quite rare are these ballot-box torches said to have been patented in 1880 to represent the ballot-boxes of that period. It was used in the parades for James G. Garfield. 4½" square by 4" high. The wick tube rises from the glass oil receptacle at the point where a real ballot-box had a slot for depositing ballots. The Smithsonian Institution gives the patentee as J. McGregor Adams of Chicago, Ill.

Many tin torches of this design were carried in processions in the campaign of 1868 when Ulysses S. Grant was elected president. The torch is 4'' in diameter and 3¾'' high. A similar torch in the Becker Collection at the Smithsonian Institution, Washington, D.C., has the names Grant and Colfax lettered on one side.

Nicely proportioned ball torch of the 1870s and 1880s. It is 3½'' in diameter and holds about one pint of burning oil.

Precious memento of a famous campaign is the McKinley-Roosevelt tin simulated lunch bucket lantern of 1900, which is in excellent condition despite its 72 years. Perforations on the other side read "Four More Years of the Full Dinner Pail," when the candlelight shines through.

Distinctly a relic of the Lincoln campaigns is this square clear glass-sided oil burning pole lantern. The frame is painted blue, now much faded. A similar lantern is in the political collection of the New York Historical Society.

carried in other parades in the first half of the century along with spectacularly ornate fire brigade pole lanterns, suggestive of the gay gondola lights of Venice and the candle pole lanterns carried in early religious processions.

In 1860 a group of Hartford, Conn., firemen organized a special Republican marching club which soon became so widely known and popular that similar units were formed in cities across the entire nation. This was the Hartford Wide Awake Club, hastily formed to serve as an escort when Abraham Lin-

coln visited Hartford to fill a speaking engagement.

Perhaps the greatest torchlight parade of all time—in point of the number of participants, at least—was the huge Lincoln Wide Awake demonstration on lower Broadway, New York, the evening of Oct. 3, 1860, in which clubs from most of the large communities of the area marched.

Globular torches made especially for the Wide Awakes predominated in the Lincoln and Grant parades. Lending variety were brass and tin eagle-shaped torches, square tin and glass pole lan-

Pierced tin lantern to hang in a window or carry in a parade at the end of a pole. To Van Buren, whose name appears on this lantern is attributed the American idiom of the designation of approval in general use today—O.K. The initials stand for Van Buren's birthplace, Old Kinderhook, N.Y.; and they have been used as an expression of approval since 1840 when they were selected as a password for the O.K. Club, a New York City Democratic organization. Anyone considered alright or approved of by the club was "O.K." with membership.

Six-sided stained glass window pole lantern, one of a matching pair from an early volunteer fire department in upstate New York. The dome and bottom have alternating red and blue panels of time-faded paint. Finials top and bottom are of brass. The yellowed woodblock print is of President Buchanan.

terns, and paper lanterns bearing pictures of the candidates.

In the rash of parades that followed the Civil War, torches took many ingenious forms. A spear-shaped torch was featured in the "Boys in Blue" parades for Rutherford B. Hayes and James G. Blaine. A globular glass torch framed in tin in simulation of the ballot box of the period was a feature of parades for Garfield in 1880; there were hat-shaped torches for Cleveland and Harrison in 1884 and 1892. In the McKinley parades in 1896 there were tin lanterns shaped like lunch buckets, with holes punched in the side so candlelight from within spelled out the names, "McKinley and Roosevelt" and the slogan, "Four More Years of the Full Dinner Pail."

Of course, it was not possible that such a fiery, fun sport could be monopolized by the grownups. The youngsters got into the act, too. For years in their play the small fry, garbed in whatever oddments of military or band uniform available or in such other fantastic parade apparel as they could devise,marched in fiery processions on the slightest excuse. If actual torches were not available, improvisations were easy. A broomstick with some rags tightly twisted about one end and held firm with hay bailing wire would, if dipped into kerosene and allowed to drain a bit before lighting, make a very impressive torch, as would a tin can stuffed with oily rags and wired or nailed to the end of a broomstick.

Juvenile torchlight parades continued into the present century well after the

Oilcloth-covered parade helmet with small nickel-plated torch on top. These, as well as a variety of caps and other military headgear, were worn in the early parades. Near the turn of the century, when parade accoutrements were becoming more sophisticated, nickel-plated helmets were worn by some marching groups. This helmet sports a Benjamin Harrison inauguration badge of 1888.

real thing had passed into history—a passing that probably resulted from Mr. Edison's genius in creating a condition that made it impossible to find Main Streets dark enough for a torchlight procession to be a novelty.

The Garfield and Hancock "Devil Dolls"

by MARIE CURIAL MENEFEE

A BOUT 1879, the author's father, Edward L. Curial, a jeweler living in Anoka, Minn., designed and patented a mechanical watch fob publicizing the presidential campaign being waged that year between James Abram Garfield and General Winfield Scott Hancock, a Civil War hero. Mr. Curial was a first class artist and engraver, consequently he designed and cut the dies for these mechanical campaign souvenirs himself. The dies were sent to a manufacturer in New York City with an initial order for 500 fobs to be finished in gold wash and nickel-plate. Curial hoped to test the market for his fobs with this small order before going into large-scale production.

The Hancock fob depicted the general in full uniform with his name across the band of his high hat; Garfield was shown in his characteristic "hands in pocket" pose; his name also was across the band of his hat. Some of the fobs were made without moving parts, some were made with a moving hand, and some were made with both moving hand and a pointed tail. Pressing down the foot of the figure

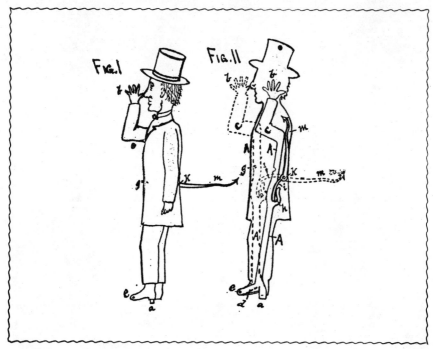

The working mechanism of E. L. Curial's watch fob was clearly defined in drawings (above) which accompanied his patent (No. 231,408), dated August 24, 1880.

on a hard surface activated the moving parts hidden between the front and back facings of the fob causing them to pop out in a most undignified gesture. A few non-mechanical pins were also produced.

The manufacturer of the watch fobs recommended to Mr. Curial that he employ street hawkers to sell these campaign trinkets so they could be demonstrated. Curial, following this advice, sent a selection of gold and nickel finished fobs to "sidewalk merchants" in various parts of the country—a hundred fobs went to a man in Philadelphia. Within a few days Mr. Curial was inundated with requests from his outlets for more fobs; many of the salesmen reported that they were literally mobbed by crowds of people wanting to buy one of his "devil dolls."

Curial sent an urgent request for more fobs to the New York manufacturer, but unfortunately the supplier's employees were out on strike at that time and he could not fill the order. By the time the strike was settled the campaign was over, and Mr. Garfield had won the election. Since only 500 of Curial's "devil doll" fobs were made, it's quite obvious that these campaign novelties are relatively rare.

A few years later, during the Blaine-Cleveland presidential campaign of 1883, similar mechanical fobs were produced — but not by Mr. Curial. Apparently his patented idea had been adopted and used by someone else.

Gold finished Garfield fobs. Left to right: Mechanical hand; non-mechanical; mechanical hand and tail; height 1 5/8".

Gold finished Hancock fobs. Left to right: Mechanical hand; non-mechanical; mechanical hand and tail; height 1 5/8".

Aeronautical Americana

by LES BEITZ

One of the exceptionally scarce "Bill Bruce" titles. As with the original display card pieces, a dust jacket in reasonably good condition calls for extra dollars when the dickering gets under way. $17.50 is not too much to pay for this "Hap" Arnold thriller in extra fine condition.

DURING THE PAST few years, an extremely avid group of buffs have been assiduously searching out and acquiring anything and everything they can latch onto in the way of memorabilia connected with early aviation. Aeronautical Americana, it's called.

Eager collectors everywhere are on the lookout for pinback buttons, tokens, badges, plaques, lapel devices and personal jewelry of like sort, statuary pieces, printed matter, novelty trinkets, accessories and all manner of paraphernalia depicting early aviators and aeroplanes—in short, every imaginable item associated with pioneer flight. Particularly "hot" at the moment is Charles A. Lindbergh material. Emphasis on this specialization is in anticipation of the 50th Anniversary of Lindy's historic solo flight from New York to Paris, coming up in June 1977.

Knowledgeable collectors are keenly aware that the value of Lindbergh items is bound to skyrocket, simply because the demand will exceed the supply.

Same goes for collectibles associated with other heroes and heroines in the annals of American aviation—Amelia Earhart, Wiley Post and Will Rogers, Commander Richard E. Byrd, "Wrong Way" Corrigan, even Howard Hughes, to mention a few. Then there are those intrepid air racers, U. S. Mail flyers, and stunt barnstormers of post-World War I era. Everything in the colorful, exciting story of early flying days and ways come into the picture.

A heavy proportion of this memorabilia, however, concerns civil aviation. Items on military aviation are just plain tough to come by. Because of the very nature of the Regular Army and its air branch, specialty houses in those days weren't afforded encouragement nor sanction in preparing and marketing trinketry depicting Army Air Corps personages and their distinctive accomplishments.

Practically nothing is available, for example, on General Billy Mitchell other than the standard magazine features (most of which is highly controversial), and a handful of miscellany in the book line—memoirs and some air-war history, mainly. But recently brought to light was an intensely interesting find dealing with pioneer military aviation—a set of six novels (yes, novels)—boys' fiction thrillers, actually, authored by General of the Army (then Major) Henry H. "Hap" Arnold!

These six classics in the field of fast-moving air adventure tales are among the most sought of all memorabilia identified with the fledgling air arm of our defense forces. Here's how it came about.

In 1927, Major Arnold and his family were stationed at Fort Riley, Kansas.

Son William attended the post school there, and in the course of his classroom work ran into more than a fair share of difficulties. As summer vacation drew near the young man's teacher suggested that William could improve his scholarship by reading more during the summer months. She recommended some boys' books—light fiction.

Now let's let Colonel William B. Arnold, USAF, pick up the story as he recalls those schooldays at Fort Riley some 46 years ago.

"My mother returned home one day with several boys' books, one of which I remember was called *The Adventure Boys In The Valley of Diamonds*. Since I was very much interested in aviation at that time, I found no interest in this fantastic story. My father said, 'Well, if you won't read that book, I'll write you one in which everything that happened is true.' And he proceeded to write *Bill Bruce and The Pioneer Aviators*.

"His method was to fill a page with type, throw it on the floor, and proceed with the next page. My mother's job was to collect these pages, put them in order, and do the editing."

The New York firm of A. L. Burt Company agreed to buy the book when it was submitted for publication, providing Major Arnold consented to prepare others to form a series built around Bill Bruce as the central character. He proceeded along that line and turned out five additional manuscripts over a 2¹/₂ month span.

The complete set of six books were published in 1928 and called The Aviation Series. They are: *Bill Bruce and the Pioneer Aviators; Bill Bruce, The Flying Cadet; Bill Bruce Becomes an Ace; Bill Bruce on the Border Patrol; Bill Bruce in the Transcontinental Race; and Bill Bruce on Forest Patrol*.

The son was delighted to have his dad do a series of books with himself, William Bruce Arnold, as the "hero"—hence, the "Bill Bruce" titles. Supporting characters in these books were named for actual Air Corps officers of the period, the spelling slightly changed in many instances. For example, Tooey Spaatz became "Tooey Spotz." The author took spe-

Machine-woven tapestry portrait in color of Charles A. Lindbergh marked on back "Made in France" and "Registered"; 18 x 18" plus selfidge. *Collection A. Christian Revi.*

cial pride in the fact that every incident involving Bill Bruce in the stories actually happened to some officer in the Army Air Corps.

Major Arnold was certainly well qualified to write about the events highlighted in those stories. He had been taught to fly by the Wright Brothers. He intimately knew and flew with the pioneers of American aviation. He was a military aviator during World War I, and in the post-war era was deeply involved in such early flight achievements as the planning and operation of the Border Patrol, Forest Patrol, and the Transcontinental Air Race.

Having plunged into the book project to help his son with his reading skills, the Commanding General of the Army Air Corps in World War II is revealed on the pages of these intriguing little

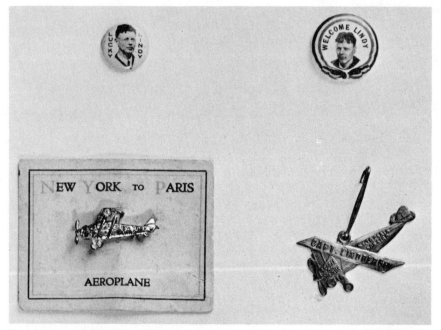

Top, left and right: Two typical pinback buttons. The smaller one, "Lucky Lindy," is a lithographed tin design which scratches quite easily and is somewhat difficult to find in fine condition. The "Welcome Lindy" celluloid button is of much better quality and usually found in near mint condition. Prices vary from $3 to $5 each. **Bottom, left and right:** Lapel pins on original display cards always command a premium price. Dealers are asking $12.50 for this "aeroplane" momento. Copper trinketry is scarce, so this much inscribed airplane ("Spirit of St. Louis" on the motor, "Capt. Lindbergh" across the wings, "New York To Paris Non Stop" along the fuselage) is a good buy at $8.50.

volumes in a warm, paternal light. Naming the series' central character after his boy was one of pride; and, of course, an extra stimulus as well.

Now something about the scarcity (and consequent value) of these six fine items of Aeronautical Americana.

If one is fortunate enough to stumble upon a complete set for $50 or thereabouts, he or she can claim membership in an elite society indeed. It's more likely, however, that the individual titles will have to be ferreted out one by one from used book shops, second hand outlets such as Goodwills and similar organizations, at rummage sales, flea markets, and similar places where discarded books are apt to appear.

The Transcontinental Air Race will prove to be the toughest to locate. Pioneer Aviators, Ace, Flying Cadet, and the Patrol titles seem to have had a good bit more impact, market-wise, selling considerably better than the air race tale.

Be that as it may, any one of the six "Hap" Arnold titles makes for an important addition to a collection of memorabilia connected with the historically important, thrill-packed days of early American flying machines and their flyers.

Playing Cards—
Collectibles Unlimited

by EDWIN C. WHITTEMORE

ILLUSTRATION A

CARD playing is a universal pastime, centuries old, but curiously, nobody knows who invented playing cards. Some say the 12th century Chinese Emperor Seun-Ho thought them up to keep his many wives busy and contented. Others claim a Gentleman of the Court of Charles VI of France created them to divert that mad monarch from melancholia. A Hindu legend attributes them to India. The Puritans assigned their origin to the Devil. The crews of Christopher Columbus' ships played cards during the sea voyage, and found American natives using painted sticks in a game similar to card games of the Far East.

Coincidence, the simultaneous unrelated birth and development of an idea without any mutual dependence whatsoever, probably accounts for this early global use of playing cards. It seems a more likely theory than that a Chinese or Indian creation was carried so immediately throughout the world by caravan, sea trade, or the Crusaders.

This widespread and long continued use of playing cards makes them, for collectors, a field of infinite variety. To work out a complete step-series system of categories for filing collections of playing cards would take the combined talents of a magician, computer programmer, library authority, and anthropologist, so endless are the variations. Many collectors start with cards of national origins — French, German, and the like—then move on to variations.

Here we can merely suggest some of the special categories which make for interesting study within the field—

ILLUSTRATION B

ILLUSTRATION C

variables in special classifications to
round out a collection already begun,
or to start a new collection on a sound
foundation.

Variations in Shape and Size. Today's standard playing card is 2¼
inches wide, 3½ inches long. For
years, it was 2½ inches by 3½ inches,
but was made narrower for easier
handling. A vast percentage of cards
are either one of these sizes. Yet now
and then, other shapes and sizes have
come into being.

In *Illustration A*, we see, left to
right: a standard 2¼ by 3½″ card;
an older, 2½ by 3½″ size, with a
special design for the poor sighted;
a round card; a narrow Chinese card;
and an odd angular-cut card.

Round cards and those with different colors for different suits seem to

be the variations most often at-
tempted by card manufacturers;
neither has made any permanent
headway. There are, of course, miniature and jumbo-sized packs of cards,
and some with curve-cut sides. Any
collection of playing cards should include examples of such variations if
only to prove the public's insistence
on the conventional rectangular card.

Variations in Card Identification.
Today's card player is well used to
immediately identifying any card by
the suit symbol and unit designation
in the upper left hand corner of the
card, as shown by the first card in
Illustration B. This is a standard
card, and a quick look at the corner
shows it to be the six of Diamonds.
The other cards in this group indicate
that quick identification was not always possible. The second in the row
is an old eight of Hearts; only by
looking carefully and mentally counting the spots does one recognize it.
Next is an early attempt to simplify
the situation by reproducing the entire card in two corners, of benefit
when cards, held in the hand, are not
seen in their entirety. Though an
improvement, the small card symbols
are not easily recognized. The last is
an early version of today's refinement
with suit symbol and numerical designation.

*Variations: Single or Double
Header?* Many steps have been taken
over the years to make the handling
of cards easier and identification
quicker. Originally there was only one
"right-side-up" to a card — for example, only one head to a Jack—and
the cards had to be arranged in the
hand accordingly. In *Illustration C,*
two cards at left are very early,
simplified "Single Headers," usable

ILLUSTRATION D

only one way up. The other two cards show two ages or steps of "Double Headers" where either end of the card may be upmost in the hand and the card is equally recognizable. The latter two also illustrate the gradual improvement in both design and reproduction through which card manufacture progressed.

Variations in Suit Symbols. Americans are pretty well used to the four standardized suit symbols — Spades, Clubs, Hearts, Diamonds—yet one of the greatest places for discovering variety in cards is in the matter of suit symbols. Incidentally, the suits (and there are usually four) can in most cases be traced back to symbolism for class distinctions.

In early Italian and Spanish cards, a sword took the place of the spade and represented nobility; a cup or chalice represented the clergy; money, the citizens; and clubs or sticks, the peasantry. The French used a lance-head for nobility, hearts for the clergy, clover for the husbandmen, and a

diamond-shaped arrowhead for the common soldier.

Illustration D shows four cards from an early German deck. The four suits seem to be bells, acorns, hearts, and leaves; their descendants today, respectively, would be Spades, Clubs, Hearts, and Diamonds. The illustrations on these particular cards are all in a series, apparently portraying a journey of conquest or adventure, perhaps a contemporary event of importance. The search for cards with colorful, imaginative, and different suit symbols is one of the great joys of card collecting.

Variations — Individual Examples. So endless are the variations in playing cards that about all one can do is to point out the types of differences and the divergence of the scope of card design as illustrated by specific examples.

In *Illustration E,* there are four such cards. First, the Ten of Stars might be called a Patriotic Card, or perhaps a Propaganda Card. It is of

ILLUSTRATION F

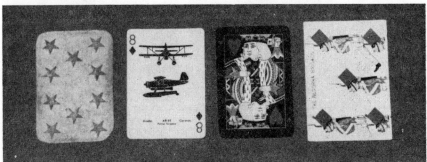

ILLUSTRATION E

Civil War vintage, produced by somebody who felt it a healthy and pleasant habit to be thinking and talking stars instead of diamonds or hearts. This style of card has never had long life. Next is an Educational Card, a type which has been successfully used on many occasions for training purposes along with recreation. This is from a training pack designed to educate plane spotters as to the outline or silhouettes of enemy planes.

The third is a simple illustration of the color-manipulation idea which has been tried and tried, but has never been permanently successful. This example is a standard card with black instead of white background. The last card is an amusing specimen from a type that is thoroughly delightful, and could almost be a subject for a collection in itself. This is known as a Transformation Card. The basic idea is to incorporate the suit symbol into an illustration—not easy to do in the multiple spot cards. This one is the five of Diamonds, with the five diamonds forming the helmets of soldiers in "The Begorra Brigade."

Variations—Oddities. Examples in *Illustration F* demonstrate more rewards in seeking the unusual and varied in playing cards, irrespective of year or nationality, or any other rigid standard of classification. First is an extremely early playing card—simple, crude and charming; the design was hand drawn and hand colored on paper, then folded over the edges of a stiffer card and glued. The second is from a deck advertising cut plug tobacco, each card showing a "pin-up girl."

The center card is from an out-and-out comic pack; the poor King has an eye patch, arm bandage, foot bandage, and cane! Next is a political card, no doubt a campaign tool, showing Grover Cleveland, candidate for President. The last card is a curious mixture — a World's Fair souvenir, combining various ideas in playing card improvements, such as the actual use of the word "ten" for quick recognition of the ten spot of Clubs, plus two types of corner spots.

Risk for the excitement of risk itself, added to man's love of entertainment and competition gives us a world where countless millions of playing cards exist. So vast are their variables that collecting them may be simple and inexpensive, or life-long, and substantial.

Collecting Old Cribbage Boards

by OTTO H. LUNDE

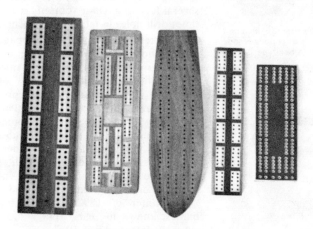

Flat cribbage boards. **Left to right:** Mahogany base veneered with walnut and maple; 12 x 3½". Various light and dark veneers; 10 x 3⅛". Solid mahogany; 12 x 3½". Mahogany base, top inlaid with maple and black walnut; 9 x 2". Eleven alternating layers of black and white bone-like materials; 7¼ x 2¾".

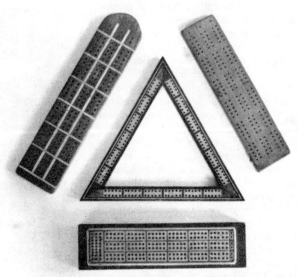

Cribbage boards for three-handed games. Left to right: 12¾ x 3"; 10¾" on all three sides; and 10½ x 2½". Bottom: 10¾ x 3".

Above: Box-type cribbage boards in open position, with inlaid designs of various woods and ivory. Below: interior of box-type boards held cards and pegs.

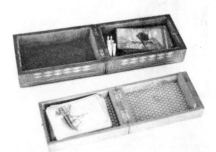

C RIBBAGE is one of the oldest card games. Its invention has been attributed to Sir John Suckling early in the seventeenth century. The cribbage board is simply a scoring board, with a surface full of holes in groups of five for easy counting, and an adequate number of scoring pegs.

Besides being a very old game, cribbage has the distinction of being unlike any other game both in the manner of play and in the system of scoring. It is simple and interesting and many consider it to be the best two-handed card game. It can also be played by three people, and by four as a partnership game. A special board is required for the three-handed game.

The speed of play and the system of scoring make it a game that can fill odd moments as well as provide lengthy entertainment. I recall a match at a rifle club where a game was continuously underway — when a player took his turn on the range another would take his place at the cribbage

table. Two games can easily be played in a half-hour lunch period.

The rules of play and scoring are easy and straightforward and are included with all new cribbage boards. They are also in card game books. New boards, available in stores today come in a great variety of shapes, sizes, and materials. Sizes vary from folding vest pocket sizes to boards several feet long. Do-it-yourselfs sometimes drill holes in tables and benches.

The real challenge in cribbage boards, however, is in collecting the numerous older types which can now be classified as antiques. Many of these are quite beautiful and represent superb craftsmanship with inlaid ivory or with marquetry which sometimes includes the suit symbols—clubs, hearts, etc. Some are also of considerable interest because of their crudity. One obviously handmade, has an inscription on the bottom which reads: "The winter of 1892 & 1893 the hardest known in years. Had a snow storm as late as April 7th."

The usual cribbage board has two rows of thirty holes and two scoring pegs for each player. There is, however, another type where every hole has a metal peg permanently placed

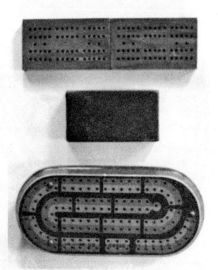

Top: A 60 point cribbage board; 7 ½ x 3 ¾"; center: Vest pocket board in closed position; bottom: Vest pocket board opened; 7 x 2".

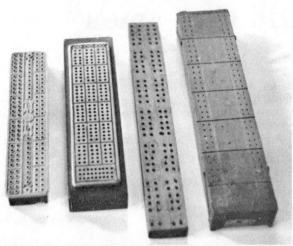

Left to right: Two cribbage boards with cast iron tops; 9¾ x 2¼" and 10¾ x 3". Two home-made cribbage boards; 14 x 2" and 14 x 3¼".

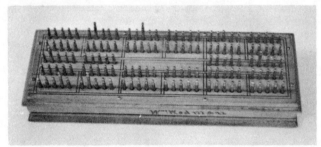

"Pull Up" cribbage board made of maple with nickel-plated brass pegs; 11 x 4 inches.

in it. To score with a particular peg it can be pulled up about half an inch. The example pictured was in extremely distressed condition when found but responded beautifully to restoration. The partially obliterated paper on the bottom revealed the following inscription: THE PERFECTION "PULL UP" CRIBBAGE BOARD AND GENERAL GAME COUNTER. TRADE MARK (The trade mark referred to a picture of the board which is only faintly discernible) MANUFACTURED AND GUARANTEED BY THE SPECIALTY CO., CORTLAND, N. Y. The Cortland County Historical Society most kindly researched the name and determined that it was a very small company which operated there for a few years around 1890.

The most common material for cribbage boards is wood but some are completely of ivory or even cast iron. Some have a cast iron top on a wood base. The simplest boards are basically flat but many are in the form of a hinged box which opens to form the flat playing surface. The box type has compartments for the scoring pegs and a deck of cards. Some of the flat types are also deep enough to have a compartment for cards and nearly all, have some provision for storing the pegs. The old pegs are usually of ivory and many of these are very finely turned. These are not readily found, however, as they were easily lost in spite of a place to store them.

As a source of entertainment cribbage has many enthusiasts. It's a relaxing game.

Old Chessmen

by ROBERT R. RADCLIFF

ONE DOES NOT have to play chess to enjoy collecting items associated with the game, but a little knowledge of chess terminology will be useful when acquiring single pieces or incomplete sets.

There are 6 basic pieces ("men") in a set of chessmen. A typical design is shown in *Figure 1*. Left to right are: Pawn, Knight, Queen, King, Bishop and Castle (or Rook). These basic pieces are combined to make a "side" of 16 men: a King, a Queen, two Bishops, two Knights, two Castles and eight Pawns. Two sides are combined to form the complete set of 32 pieces. Generally, the sides differ only in color, such as red and white or black and white, and the designs of the basic pieces are the same throughout.

Collectors of old chessmen are usually disappointed when they encounter poorly matched sets, incomplete sets, or single pieces. Unfortunately, these situations often occur, for rarely do matched pieces of any game survive 100 or 200 years without breakage or loss. Small wonder that 18th and 19th century ivory, bone, or wood chess sets with 32 perfectly matched pieces in perfect condition are scarce and expensive!

In his authoriatative *Book of Chessmen,* the late Alex Hammond offered these pithy comments on our subject: ". . . the possession of single pieces, no matter how beautiful or famous they may be, is always a source of dissatisfaction; one wonders where the other pieces are, if they are still in existence and whether they will ever come one's way. Although one may spend years happily chasing the missing pieces, this feeling of frustration always prevails, in addition to which one's friends or relations who view these 'remnants' are sure to voice the opinion that it is a pity the set should be short of so many pieces . . . "

Despite Hammond's opinions, interest is increasing in collecting single chess pieces or incomplete sets, for this way, at reasonable cost, one can specialize in specimens illustrating various designs, various materials of construction such as ivory or wood, various colors such as white, red, or green, and various sizes from miniatures to gigantic. Some specialists collect only Kings and Queens for these usually have the best craftsmanship and largest dimensions. Others prefer Knights, Bishops, or Castles.

With no feeling of frustration, I enjoy "happily chasing the missing pieces" deplored by Hammond. Admittedly, flea markets and shops are scoured many times to uncover a few items. At other times only broken pieces needing extensive restoration can be found. Sometimes one feels fortunate to accumulate the 6 basic pieces from a particularly attractive or unusual set, knowing that there is little chance for completing it.

A collection of chess pieces can begin with the black basalt King and Queen shown in *Figure 2*. These striking 5-inch figural pieces were designed by Wedgwood and are currently available from most shops selling their wares.

Another King and Queen combination, also about 5-inches high, is shown in *Figure 3*. These are traditional English pieces, circa 1810, of turned and carved bone, usually found in natural and red colors.

Next to Kings and Queens, Knights from old sets are probably collected most often. *Figure 4* shows three examples of good work. Left to right, the men are from an English set circa 1825, a Dutch set circa 1800, and a standard English design circa 1850. The tallest piece is 2³/4 inches.

Castles are interesting collectibles, particularly the 19th century flagged varieties shown in *Figure 5*. On the left is a traditional English version, on the right a well-carved Chinese or Indian type 4 inches tall. Note the "Union Jack" flag on the latter.

Fig. 1

Fig. 2

Fig. 3

Fig. 4

Fig. 7

Fig. 6

Fig. 5

Bishops occur in many variations. The unusually large (4 inches tall) figural type shown in *Figure 6* was carved about 1800 from solid ivory.

Even the lowly Pawns can have good design and workmanship, as shown in *Figure 7*. These four 19th century examples are, left to right: Dutch, Indian; French (?); and English. The tallest is 2½ inches.

The six pieces in *Figure 8* are from an early 19th century French (Dieppe) bone set of an interesting design. The King is 4½ inches tall. The pieces break easily, for they are delicate and are assembled from small components. Many hundreds of these sets were made and pieces can still be found, although complete sets in perfect condition are rare. Collecting a complete set offers a worthy challenge.

Fig. 8

Collecting Lead Soldiers

by PETER JOHNSON

William Britain's horse ambulance of the Royal Army Medical Corps; a rare version in service dress from the early part of the First World War.

The Village Idiot (left), one of the rarest of Britain's single figures, said to have owed his origin to a remark made by Queen Mary, consort of King George V. Milkman (center) with cart containing tiny milk cans. Village Blacksmith (right) with his anvil. All figures are about 2¼" tall.

IF A. A. MILNE were to pen his famous children's poem today—rhymes notwithstanding—he might be forgiven for writing: *They're changing the guard at Jackson Heights . . .* or *Glenview, Ill.* Or *Hanover, Pa.,* for that matter. For, in truth, a vast army of soldiers which changed the guard in Christopher Robin's nursery—and in countless other British homes—is crossing the Atlantic in ever-growing volume.

Old lead soldiers are the target of a specialized and discriminating band of American collectors who are investing in nostalgia to a degree which has rocketed the penny toy soldier to astronomic heights of value.

Take the case of the Montenegrin infantry. Around the outbreak of the First World War, the premier firm of British toy soldier manufacturers, aptly named William Britain, issued sets of eight

Britain's figures of townspeople; civilian figures are highly sought-after by collectors as they were made in much fewer numbers than the soldiers. (N.B. This doees not necessarily refer to farm figures.)

gray-uniformed troops of this Balkan state in graphically decorated boxes adorned with shiny red paper. The price per box was one shilling, or 13 cents at today's rates. An American collector recently bought such a set at auction in London for $52, an appreciation of 40,000 per cent. (Beat that on the stock market if you can!)

The last seven years have been the most significant steps in toy soldier collecting. Primarily one must distinguish between the custom-built model figures of present day makers, intricate works of art appealing to the collector who demands accuracy rather than age, and the lead toys of yesterday. When the firm of Britain's stopped producing in lead seven years ago, the soldiers we, our fathers and grandfathers had as

children were assured of a place as collectors' items.

But the story really begins in 1893. Until then, the lead soldier market was dominated by the Germans and, to a lesser extent, the French. Their products were heavy, solid figures, well made and painted but relatively expensive in their consumption of lead. William Britain, whose family had made mechanical toys from the early 19th century, created a revolution in nursery warfare by introducing a hollow-cast soldier which was to lead the world market for the next 70 years.

Old Mr. Britain sent one of his sons along to Gamages, a huge, Victorian department store renowned for its perspicacity in spotting a commercial winner. Gamages agreed to try the new

Left to right: Farm couple seated on lead bench; Milkmaid milking a red and white cow (3" long by 2" high); farm woman carrying a basket and umbrella (2¼" tall).

Britain's soldiers, the first of which were 54mm Life Guards, resplendent in their red tunics, gleaming cuirasses, and white plumes. (Incidentally, the same uniformed troops are a tourist eye-catcher in Royal London to this day.) At a few pence a box they sold well and Gamages were soon at Mr. Britain's door asking for more. The whole family joined in with gusto, the men designing and casting and the daughters painting and packing the soldiers.

As the cheaply produced, yet accurate, hollow-cast figures undercut all other lines, Britain's were able to extend their production and soon hundreds of thousands of basic figures were being fed into a cottage industry in which working class families, issued with enamels, brushes, and instruction charts, earned themselves a modest income by hand-painting the models.

In time practically every regiment in the British army appeared in the Britain catalog—hence the dominance of scarlet-coated figures in any representative collection today. The armies of other countries had their place, however, as Britain's were swift to react whenever and wherever a conflict broke out in the world.

The South African War led to the introduction of Boer infantry and cavalry; a rash of minor Balkan flare-ups brought obscure uniforms on the scene; Japanese and Russians faced each other in miniature warfare in 1904.

When the United States fought in

Coronation Coach (20" long); coach and horse trappings gilded; riders in red and white livery.

A splendid, 22-man band of the Royal Marine Light Infantry, made by William Britain. A rare set of a regiment which went out of existence earlier this century; $156.

Farm Waggon (9" long) from Home Farm Series, by W. Britain, ca. 1905. Drover to the side of the wagon stands 2¼" tall. Wooden crates and barrels fill the wagon.

Right: Sir Walter Woodland, banner bearer to the Black Prince, on prancing horse. **Left:** Sir Howell y Fwyall, on foot, with Wessex Dragon standard; $68.

German Elastolin figures of the Nazis, made in a composition material; they represented Hess (two figures on left), Goering, Hitler saluting, and two figures of Hindenburg; $78.

"Edward, The Black Prince"; a Coutenay figure; $98.

Horse Roller (5¼" long) from the Home Farm Series, by W. Britain. Registry No. 459993 indicates this design was registered at the London Patent Office's Design Registry in 1905. Original box in background.

Cuba, Britain's drafted American infantry with bayonets at the ready, led by a dashing officer holding pistol and sword. To face them were colorful Spanish infantry and trotting cavalry.

The figure of the American infantry was adapted from an earlier British soldier, the slouch-hatted City Imperial Volunteer of London. Much later, in the 1950s, the figures were to undergo another adaptation and re-emerge as Union and Confederate troops.

Production was by no means confined to the military. Railroad personnel and the band of the Salvation Army with its long-skirted women officers is today highly prized by collectors on both sides of the Atlantic.

As a reaction to the militarism of the First World War, Britain's introduced their Home Farms series in the 1920s. From this came one of their greatest rarities. It is said that Queen Mary, the Consort of King George V, on being shown one of the farm and village collections with dozens of minute figures, animals, and implements, remarked: "Surely, the village idiot is missing."

Britain's rectified the omission and the village idiot, straw in mouth, duly appeared in the catalog. He had only a short life, however, thereby guaranteeing a high price on his head should he turn up today in some dusty cellar!

Britain's prolific output has placed their models in the van for model soldier societies throughout the world. Phillips, the London fine art auctioneers, hold four sales a year entirely devoted to lead soldiers, most of them Britain's, and on the occasion of such a sale an army of 10,000 figures goes under the auctioneer's hammer. It is estimated that half of any sale finally makes its way across the Atlantic to American collectors.

The paucity of good U. S.-made lead toy soldiers—and again, I differentiate from the many excellent contemporary models made for the connoisseur collector in the States—has focused attention on the British market. Several American military enthusiasts make trips to Europe in search of Britain's models for their collections. One such is the executive of a chain of drive-in restaurants on the West Coast. His ambition used to be to own as many soldiers as drive-ins—2,000 of them. He has long since passed his target, but is still a regular visitor to London in pursuance of his hobby.

German and French manufacturers have their place in soldier collecting. Heyde, a famous old German firm which made solids throughout the 19th century and into the 20th, had an enormous range of figures. Their models often included intricate tableaux of soldiers engaged in various activities, such as setting up bivouac, bridge-building and operating field kitchens.

Another make, Elastolin, under which mark are still produced plastic historical figures, siege weapons, and Wild West sets, is sought after for Nazi-era figures which included Hitler and his henchmen, as well as hundreds of different Wehrmacht models, correct in every detail.

They were made in the 1930s in a composition material—it deteriorates with damp—and even included dead men and horses for battleground realism. The general holocaust of war in Germany and subsequent de-Nazification led to their scarcity and consequent collectors' demand. An Elastolin figure of Hitler with spring-loaded saluting arm can command as much as $20 today.

Mignot and Lucotte, French makers, produced solids covering scores of battle-honored French regiments. Massed groups of cavalry, sometimes to be seen in expensive militaria shops of Paris, evoke the old glories of the French Army as no other figures can. Many fine examples of these figures are to be seen in the Musée de L'Armee at Les Invalides, Paris.

Visitors to London will find model soldiers deployed in fascinating dioramas at the Imperial War Museum which deals with the two world wars and beyond, and at the National Army Museum in Chelsea, which tells the story of the British Army up to 1914. A stone's throw from the latter museum, a specialist dealer in a large, indoor antiques market, who caters to the lead soldier collector offers a wide range of Britain's old models at all prices. (The Lead Soldier, Stall No. N3, Antiquarius, 135 King's Road, London SW3.) In the West End of London, Tradition at 188 Piccadilly, W1, stocks new and old models for the collector, books, and other militaria.

Buddy "L" Toys Prior to 1930

by EMMA STILES

IMPRESSIVE, indeed—those mighty steel Buddy "L's" that rode high wide and handsome through the Depression era. Highly detailed, ultimate in realism, true scale model Buddy "L" toys, famous the world over for quality construction, were the very first heavy gauge steel playthings. Prior to this metal toys were heavy brittle cast iron or light weight metals.

Buddy "L" toys were invented and developed shortly after the first decade of the 19th century by Fred A. Lundahl, owner of the Moline Pressed Steel Corporation, Moline, Illinois, manufacturer of heavy steel automobile fenders and other auto p_rts.

Buddy "L" Flivver Delivery, No. 210. Chassis is regular Ford design, steel frame, steel axles, aluminum wheels, auto-type steering mechanism, crown fenders, streamline hood and regulation Ford roadster body with one-man top. Black with red wheels, 12½" long, 5¾" wide, 7" high. Weight 3 lbs.

Lundahl one day brought home a toy size model of a real dump truck which he had made for his son out of scrap fender parts. The dump truck was realistic; it really worked. Lundahl's son loved it and played with it all the time. The following Christmas Lundahl's son received another steel toy, a scale model operating steam shovel that really scooped, also handmade by his Dad.

Lundahl called the toys "Buddy" after his son whose real name was Arthur, but whose family and friends called him "Buddy." The "L" was added when several other "Buddy's" moved into the neighborhood, and Lundahl's son became known as "Buddy 'L.' "

When Lundahl's neighbors saw the rugged durability of these true to life indestructible all steel toys, they asked for toys like Buddy L's. Lundahl soon had more orders than he could handle.

Later, on the advice of friends, he showed Buddy "L" toys to the buyer of the F. A. O. Schwarz toy store in New York City. He immediately received a substantial order. The day he visited Marshall Field in Chicago, the buyer there gave him an equally large order. Now Buddy "L" toys were in business.

During the 1920s, Buddy "L" featured a complete line of deluxe model construction equipment. So realistic

Buddy "L" Steam Shovel, Model 220, black with red truck platform and cab roof. 25" long, 10" wide, 14" high. Weight 8 lbs. Model 220-A is an improved version, slightly larger, weighing 17 lbs. Model 220-AB is same construction but equipped with traction truck, 14" long with 3" wheels, steel axles and crawler-type tread made of steel link chain sections. It is 27½" long, 17" high, 12" wide and weighs 18 lbs.

Buddy "L" Hydraulic Aerial Truck, bright red with nickel trim. Ladder unit, of steel sectional type, can be extended to 4½ feet by means of cable windlass which is provided with safety locks. Weight 15 lbs.

was each toy that boys could carry out, in miniature, projects they most admired in the workaday world; also Buddy "L" playthings were designed to become the media of play for an entire group. Therein lay the secret, from the very beginning, of the nationwide popularity of Buddy "L" all steel playthings. They are now becoming rather scarce and of increasing historical interest.

These big road-building, earthmoving playthings are remarkable reproductions in miniature of man-size machines, designed not only to look like the big ones, but to actually work like them. They are the most spectacular operating action toy ever created. They do everything the real construction equipment does. They convey and elevate, scoop, claw and dig, lift, swing, haul; they grade, shovel, push, pull, mix, carry, and dump.

The Buddy "L" Sand Loaders have buckets mounted on an endless chain which, when operated by crank, actually scoop up the sand from the pile and elevate it to the top where it is dumped into a chute and spouted into waiting trucks.

Buddy "L" Sand Screener is a complete sand and gravel plant consisting of truck, elevator, chute, screen, measuring bin, and hopper.

Buddy "L" Traveling Crane is a reproduction of the big cranes used for handling heavy objects in plants and quarries, etc.

Buddy "L" Aerial Tower Tramway is copied after the large tramways used to convey materials over streams, ravines, wooded plots, and other obstacles between two points.

Buddy "L" Small Derrick duplicates the derrick which building contractors used to lift things around and save manpower.

Buddy "L" Big Derrick is copied from the large power derricks used for handling coal, ashes, sand, gravel and other materials from piles to truck, or for loading or unloading cars, barges, etc.

Buddy "L" Stream Dredge looks and works like the big machines that are used for dredging canals, rivers, lakes.

Buddy "L" Tractor Dredge is a reproduction of a steam dredge fitted with crawler treads to prevent miring in low swampy sections.

Buddy "L" Hoisting Tower, one of the most unusual playthings ever produced, is an exact miniature working model of the hoisting towers used on large construction jobs for spouting mixed concrete to the various parts of the job.

Buddy "L" Road Roller is a remarkable reproduction by Buddy "L"

Buddy "L" Oil Truck; cab is black, tank and body green. Comes with four special oil cans for can racks on sides of truck. 25½" long, 12½" high, 8½" wide. Weight 13 lbs.

engineers of the big steam rollers used on street and highway work throughout the country.

Buddy "L" Steam Shovel is a faithful replica of the big fellows that dig into the earth.

Buddy "L" Trench Digger digs and elevates dirt into a conveyor which carries it onto piles or loads it into trucks.

Buddy "L" Concrete Mixer, identical to the big ones used on bridges, dams, roads, etc., really mixes cement. Buddy "L" also made concrete mixers fitted with crawler type traction wheels.

The Buddy "L" Railroad featured throughout the 1920s is one of the greatest of all outdoor playthings. It is

Buddy "L" Moving Van. Bright green body; red chasis; hood, fenders and seat are black. Panel type body with inside loading space; 2 hinged doors at rear. Top of body forms canopy over driver's seat. 25" long, 12½" high, 8½" wide. Weight 11 lbs.

scarce now, and is considered a first class collector's item in the heavy steel toy category. This model locomotive is a faithful reproduction of the big compounders used in fast freight service. The locomotive tender is built just like the big engine tenders with water tank; the box car is regular merchandise type; the dump car, hopper type. The Tank Car is built just like the big cars for hauling liquids of all kinds. The Flat Car is fitted with stake sockets. The Stock Car is reproduced exactly like the regular standard livestock cars. The Coal Car is gondola type.

The Locomotive Wrecking Crane is copied after the big ones; and the Locomotive Dredge is an exact reproduction of the big outfits. The Caboose is built with regulation cupola, front and rear platform, and is completely fitted with ladders, hinged doors, and guard rails. The all steel track sections have 15 ties, are 7 feet long and 4 inches wide. The tracks are also quite scarce.

Buddy "L" made at this period an Industrial Train which was much smaller. Whereas the cars of the big train measured 20 inches or more, those of the Industrial Train averaged 8 inches. The tracks belonging to the Industrial Train are 24 inch sections, 4 inches wide.

While all Buddy "L" toys prior to

1930 are eagerly sought and highly regarded by the collector, the most desirable of the automotive are the Ford Flivver Line, exact reproductions of the famous Model T Ford, duplicated in every detail.

The Flivver line included: Buddy "L" Flivver Delivery—the model that darted throughout the 1920s here, there, and everywhere, delivering meats, groceries, dry goods, notions, and what nots; Buddy "L" Flivver Coupe—copy of the famous Model T Ford Coupe; Buddy "L" Ford Dump Cart—used extensively on construction work for hauling concrete, cinders, and other material; Buddy "L" Ford Dump Truck—used on construction jobs; Buddy "L" One Ton Ford Delivery Truck—well known the country over; Buddy "L" One Ton Ford Express—another excellent likeness of a famous product.

Most all fire fighting toys seem to rate high with collectors. Any Buddy "L" fire fighting apparatus, with realism action, is a worthwhile addition to a collection. To look for are: Buddy "L" Fire Engine—equipment is very real in appearance; Buddy "L" Fire Truck—equipped with two extension ladders, fire gong and hose reel with 20 feet of cord hose; Buddy "L" Hydraulic Aerial Truck—the most spectacular model in the Buddy "L" line—it stands 56 inches tall with ladders extended; Buddy "L" Insurance

Buddy "L" Hoisting Tower, No. 350, 39" high, base 12" square. Weight 22½ lbs. Green with black buckets and spouts. Loading skip at base is filled with mixed cement; loader hoist raises it to highest point on the track where it is tilted and emptied into bucket inside tower framework. A second hoist then raises bucket to desired tower height where cement is emptied into a large hopper from which it is poured from any of the 3 faucets right into the forms.

Buddy "L" Flivver Coupe, No. 210-B. True to life chassis with all doors, openings, rear compartments, etc. in exact detail. Black with red wheels. 12" long, 5¾" wide, 7" high. Weight 3 lbs.

Patrol—which goes to the fires, with other apparatus, for the purpose of protecting furniture and other goods from damage by water.

Greatly in demand are those fabulous Buddy "L" deluxe model delivery trucks of the 1920s, identical in quality of material and workmanship to the local trucks built expressly for hauling. These models are: Buddy "L" Express Truck—the original Buddy "L" toy, the model that held the weight of a 200 pound man and established the fame of the Buddy "L" name; Buddy "L" Dump Truck—that really dumped; Buddy "L" Hydraulic Dump Truck—that looks and works like the man-size trucks; Buddy "L" Coal Truck—built like big city coal trucks used in hauling coal delivered by chute through sidewalk or basement openings; Buddy "L" Sand and Gravel Truck for sand and gravel delivery—body has removable partitions for separate loads; Buddy "L" Oil Truck—can racks on each side of tank hold four removable special oil cans.

Other trucks in the line are: Buddy "L" Ice Truck—equipment includes pair steel ice tongs and three pieces of glass imitation ice; Buddy "L" Lumber Truck—body is stake platform type; Buddy "L" Baggage Truck—complete with baggage equipment; Buddy "L" Moving Van—top of body forms a protective canopy over driver's seat; Buddy "L" Railway Express Truck; Buddy "L" Street Sprinkler—tank has large filler cap and brass faucets which feed water into a sprinkler bar perforated with holes the entire length.

Buddy "L" also made an Auto Wrecker, with automotive-type crane, to keep the rest of the fleet rolling.

During the 1920s Buddy "L" manufactured a coach fitted with two rows of steel coach chairs.

A prime favorite for the collectors of Buddy "L" toys would be a Tug Boat, if you could be fortunate enough to obtain one. Buddy "L" tug boats actually run—by air motor. The speed is governed by a regulating valve on the stern deck.

Another rare addition to a Buddy "L" collection would be a monoplane. Few people today realize that Buddy "L," prior to 1930, made a monoplane, "The Lone Eagle," an exact copy of the popular cabin-type, fast, long-distance air cruisers, every feature faithfully duplicated.

The deluxe model automotive toys of the 1920s closely followed motor car design. Truck frames were fabricated from special automobile steel channel sections. Bodies were of 20 gauge automobile steel, steering mechanism of the automobile type. The narrowed front end provided shorter turning radius for the wheels.

Truck wheels were of one solid piece, number 12 cast aluminum metal with hubs drilled in the center of the wheel and fitted with oil-less wood bearings, the same as in expensive electrical machinery. The polished circumference gave the rubber tire effect to the wheels.

The deluxe model playthings of the

Buddy "L" Sand Loader, olive green, trimmed in black and red. Overall 21" long, 9½" wide, 18" high. A special feature is the mechanism consisting of hand wheel, rack and gear which permits changing the pitch of the elevator so that it will work low or high on the sand pile as desired.

Buddy "L" Concrete Mixer, No. 280, grey—all colors are baked-on enamel. An all steel measuring shovel came with each machine. 23" long, 17½" wide with skip down, 17½" high. Weight 16½ lbs. Model No. 280-A operates the same but truck is fitted with crawler-type traction wheels. Dimensions differ only slightly.

Buddy "L" Outdoor Railroad. The greatest of all playthings. Photo by Adam Kierst, South Amboy, N.J.

1920s were given a hard, lasting, lustrous finish by dipping in two coats of automobile enamel. Each coat was thoroughly baked on in massive ovens where the heat was constantly maintained at high temperatures to provide a wear-resisting surface. The colors were designed to look like those of the man-sized machines they represented.

All construction equipment bore the familiar orange, yellow, and dark green commonly used on all big machines. Most prominent of the Ford line, as well as the delivery fleet, were black with red trim. Exceptions were the oil truck, where tank and body were green; the body of the baggage and ice truck, which was yellow; the tank on the street sprinkler, a green; and the moving van which was bright green. The fire fighting apparatus was, of course, a brilliant red.

The size of the 1920 deluxe model Buddy "L" playthings is almost unbelievable. Most measured 2 feet or more in length, with the exception of the Ford Flivver line which measured 12 inches. The locomotive and tender, with cars coupled together, actually measured 22 feet. The Hydraulic Aerial Truck was 39 inches long and 56 inches tall with ladder extended.

The Traveling Crane was 46 inches long, 33 inches high overall. The Aerial Tram was 33 inches tall; the Steam Dredge, 33 inches long with boom lowered; and the Hoisting Tower, 39 inches tall.

Some of the deluxe model Buddy "L" construction equipment of the 1920s actually weighed more than its child operator. The Sand Screener, Traveling Crane, and Hoisting Tower each weighed 22 pounds, the Aerial Tramway, 32 pounds, and the Trench Digger an unbelievable 42 pounds.

The price of Buddy "L" deluxe toys was quite astounding for depression times. For quality, accuracy and, above all, the ability to outlast several generations of husky youngsters, customers paid the price. Delivery trucks averaged $7 to $9. Cement mixers were listed at $15.

Many of these fabulous deluxe models of the 1920s which were comparatively larger and more elaborate than the junior line introduced in the 1930s are becoming difficult to locate and obtain. However, it is still possible for anyone who wishes to specialize in this field to gather an interesting and worthwhile collection.

Outstanding Mettlach Steins

From the Collection of
GEORGE M. BLEEKMAN

2140/952 — Porcelain becher, print under glaze. Boy on bicycle waves at steam train. Multicolor. ½ L. The number 2140 refers to the plain steins used for prints under glaze.

IN ONE of the most charming spots in the beautiful Rhine country, where the Moselle takes the waters of the Saar, the Sons of St. Benedict, some twelve hundred years ago, built the Abbey of Mediolacum. The name, meaning "between the lakes," eventually became Mettlach. Through the centuries the Abbey grew in size and importance. Time after time enemies sought to destroy it. Patiently the monks rebuilt. But with the French Revolution, the monks were finally driven out, the monastery plundered, and the lands confiscated or sold.

In 1809, Eugene Francis Boch, through purchase from the govern-

ment, came into possession of the ruins and the lands. Only the ivy clad chapel, known as the "Old Tower," stood as a reminder of past glories. Boch's purpose was to found a pottery —a business he had learned at his father's establishment at Sept Fontaines, near Luxemburg.

His early difficulties were many. The region abounded in hard coal, and the Government had set as a condition of sale that hard coal should be used in firing the Boch kilns. Up to then, wood firing was the accepted method, and Boch had to develop new techniques. His pottery at Mettlach was the first to introduce coal firing

Top row, left to right:

1648 — Gray pottery; design resembles tapestry panel "tacked on." Reads: When your sweetheart gives you sorrow, take a tankard to your heart. ½ L.

1452—Etched design, ½L. One of a set used with master stein #1492.

Bottom row, left to right:

2090 — Etched pottery beecher, showing man with Bavarian pipe, cards, etc. Reads: The worse the wife, the better the bar; the better the bar, the worse the wife. Lid shows cow jumping over moon. Multicolor. ½ L.

2034—Etched design of white diamonds bordered with gold on delicate blue ground. ½ L.

2191—Etched, humorous scene, Roman officer saluting guard oblivious of girl in guardhouse. Latin inscription. Top, brown, base, brown-black; people, in white; gold trim. ½ L.

in the kilns of Europe. The second to follow in this practice was the neighboring factory at Wallerfangen, which Nicholas Villeroy had founded in 1789. In 1836, Villeroy was to unite with Boch in a joint enterprise.

Boch also introduced a water power system for turning lathes and potters' wheels—foot operations from earliest times.

The first marketable pieces he produced were a soft calciferous body, but these were soon displaced by a hard bodied earthenware which eventually equalled English ironstone.

The Mettlach establishment became a paradise for artisans and workers in

1816—Mosaic, floral decoration on bulbous body. 3/10 L.

2001—Book stein, glazed. Panel design shows backs of famous theological texts; name of priest from monastery in Wartburg, presumably its owner, inscribed on inner side of lid. ¼ L. Similar steins, with the same number, show books of other professions, as medicine, law, etc.

ceramics. The company supplied housing and offered training in pottery production. A large colony of capable workers grew up around the Old Abbey. New forms and models and more distinctive ornamentations were developed. Old stoneware methods were studied and newer techniques applied to old designs.

By 1851 the Old Abbey was completely restored to its original form and the old Benedictine motto, *Ecce Labora,* once again was carved over the entrance. The Old Tower was used as the incised mark on Mettlach wares.

2767—Etched. "Child of Munich" placing bung in beer keg; wall at base in low relief; famous Frauenkirke with twin spires in background. Pewter top with Munich coat of arms on thumb lift. Multicolor. ½ L.

V & B Expansion

Between 1836 and 1840, several factories in the Saar Basin were consolidated under the management of Villeroy & Boch. These included the potteries at Sept Fontaines (founded 1766), Wallerfangen, Mettlach, and Schramberg (founded 1820).

Later, other factories were added to the Villeroy & Boch chain: in 1856, at Dresden, originated by V & B; in 1879, a crystal glassworks at Wadgassen (founded 1841), and a terra cotta factory at Merzig (founded 1841). Still later acquisitions were a new tile factory at Danischburg in 1906-07; earthenware factories at Bonn, in 1919; a mosaic tile works at Deutsch-Lissa in 1920; and a new earthen works, built at Torgau on Elbe in 1926.

With so many factories to produce, Villeroy & Boch has, over the years, put out a great variety of wares, with varying marks. Of them all, their steins made at Mettlach are most widely known today.

Inlaid Stone Ware

In 1860, at Mettlach, a ware known as "Chromolith" was developed. In this, the ornamentation, instead of being in bas relief, was inlaid into the body of the articles in colored clays in various designs, giving somewhat the effect of cloisonne enamel work. This was the beginning of their inlaid ware for commercial purposes. It was orig-

3194 — Royal blue ground; white cameo-like Piper figure. ½ L.

1740—Relief design in white on tan ground. ½ L.

inal in conception, and the secret of the colored clays was withheld from competition.

The first pieces consisted of steins, tankards, and chalices. The initial costs of the ware were prohibitive, but steady improvement in methods eventually brought it to market. As Mettlach's Inlaid Stone Ware, it captured public fancy. In this country it was awarded a Grand Prix at the Philadelphia Centennial in 1876, at the Chicago World's Fair in 1893, and at the St. Louis Fair in 1904.

By the beginning of the 20th century, new items, in addition to the popular steins, were being introduced in the ware. An advertisement in *McClure's Magazine*, April, 1909, announced that all the better retail shops through the United States were offering "Mettlach Steins, Tankards, Wall Plaques, Vases, Punch Bowls, Jardinieres and Pedestals, Tobacco Jars, etc., done in Inlaid Colored

Clays, likewise in Bas-Relief, Printed and Hand-Painted Under-glaze Decoration." [Print under-glaze on stoneware, from specially designed copper plates, was another Mettlach · first, and sets consisting of one large 3-liter stein with 6 or 12 matching beakers or tumblers in ¼-liter size were extremely popular.]

In addition to the above, tea sets, toilet sets, and umbrella stands were made in the Inlaid Stoneware, and just before 1914 when production of this ware stopped, tablewares were introduced.

The End of Mettlach

In 1921 the works at Mettlach were destroyed by fire, together with the main office, and the museum. All important documents and records went up in flames. Production at Mettlach was never resumed. No steins (or other pieces, for that matter) have been made with the familiar Mettlach castle mark since that date.

It is known that Villeroy & Boch issued catalogues of their Mettlach

2141—Etched. View of University town of Tubingen. Multicolor. ½ L.

wares prior to 1890; one of 30-pages in 1894; a master catalogue in 1899 which listed and pictured wares then in production, (many had been continued for years); and one in 1901. All of these belonging to the company, with the original photographs and drawings of the steins in them, were lost in the fire of 1921.

The catalogues, which are printed in German, evidently had little distribution in this country. Antiques Publications, in Taneytown, Maryland, owns one of the 1899 editions, and some years ago, made up photostat pages for sale. Mrs. Marjorie M. Smith, also of Taneytown, has in her collection one of the 1901 issues. There may be others about, but they are rare indeed.

In his paperbound *Mettlach Steins and Their Prices,* R. H. Mohr has apparently utilized either the 1899 catalogue or a facsimile of it to describe, though not picture, the numbered steins in it (6 through 3142). Not all the numbers appear in the catalogue; presumably they were not in production when the catalogue was issued, or were introduced after it was published or perhaps were never used at all.

Actual pictures of Mettlach steins, which collectors like very much to have, must be sought from collector sources, and information on pieces not contained in the catalogues is particularly welcome.

Mr. George M. Bleekman, Jr. of the Department of Biology at the University of Oregon in Eugene, taught from 1958 to 1964 at the Ludwigsburg American High School in Germany. There he began to collect Mettlach products, chiefly steins, and he brought back some 27 official pieces (marked and numbered) and five or more unmarked pieces of recognizable Mettlach quality.

The pieces pictured here are from his collection. All are numbered and bear the Mettlach Old Tower mark. Descriptions were furnished by Mr. Bleekman.

Jolly Old Effigy Nutcrackers Now Collectors' Treasures

by SAM A. COUSLEY

1

2

3

ONE OF THE ALL-TIME popular fairy tales associated with Christmas for more than a century, is the whimsical story, "The Nutcracker and the Mouse King," written by E. T. A. Hoffman in 1840. It was Dumas' adaptation of this story which inspired Tchaikovsky to compose his celebrated "Nutcracker Suite," first performed in St. Petersburg in 1892 as the feature of a Christmas festival.

The fantasy tells the story of a little girl whose favorite of her Yule presents was a nutcracker in the form of a sol-

4

who promptly persuaded Clara to accompany him to the delightful Fairy Kingdom where they were entertained by sugar plum fairies and other fanciful creatures.

From time immemorial the cracking and eating of nuts around an open fire has been traditional Christmas fun and generally a jolly, sociable Winter pastime—particularly so in days of old when life was simple and amusements few and homespun. Wherever the custom of hanging up Christmas stockings has prevailed, nuts always have been among the staple "stocking fillers."

6

5

Nut meats ever have been an important ingredient of Yule plum puddings, fruit cakes, cookies, candies and other seasonal dainties.

It is only natural, therefore, that in many countries—particularly in Europe—nutcrackers have been popular and appropriate gifts for grownups and children alike, and they have been cast or hand-wrought in brass, bronze, iron, and silver, and carved in hardwoods in infinite imaginative forms. Back in the 15th century Chaucer mentioned nutcrackers in his *Canterbury Tales,* and in the 16th century, Henry VIII, it is recorded, gave one to Ann Boleyn as a birthday gift.

In the north of England Halloween is known as Nutcrack Night, and nuts play as important a part as apples in the games and pastimes which are tradi-

dierly character with massive jaws. When the Christmas guests had gone and the family was asleep, little Clara dreamed that her gifts had come to life and were being attacked by an army of mice.

The Nutcracker was losing a duel with the Mouse King when Clara intervened and threw her slipper at the mouse. Suddenly the nutcracker was transformed into a handsome prince

which were too hard to crack with the teeth. Many delicious nuts fall into this class—the American hickory nuts, the black walnut, the butternut, the Brazil nut, some pecans, hazel nuts, and Hawaiian macadamia nuts.

7

tional customs of the occasion.

In America 60 to 100 years ago, nutting parties were popular Fall outings. Many varieties of nuts grew in such abundance that in some parts of the country farmers on whose land the trees grew regarded them as practically worthless and freely gave permission for nutting parties to gather them. It has only been since about 1900 that nuts —principally pecans, hazel nuts, and walnuts—have been comercially grown in this country.

The first nutcrackers were utilitarian little machines designed solely for the job of breaking the shells of edible nuts

10

8   9

Primitive man, no doubt, solved the problem of hard shells by bashing them between stones, but with the iron age came the invention of various lever-type crackers which came down through the years to take their place as important household or personal implements. These, as their functional features were improved to a point approaching perfection, then began to assume more pleasing and ornamental shapes. In the 17th, 18th, and 19th centuries nutcracker design stressed ornamentation so much they practically developed into an art form. When that happened they commanded the attention of collectors who now seek them as beautiful and novel trinkets with an importance entirely aside from their practical purpose.

The nutcrackers in the Cousley Historical Collections of Englewood, N. J., are of this sort. Gathered over a long period of years from around the world, some are the products of the famous wood carvers of Germany's Black Forest and the Swiss Alps. Others are from France, England, Italy, Russia, and Asiatic countries. They take the form of dogs, lions, deer, squirrels, eagles, roosters, elephants, alligators, and other interesting animals in hardwoods and metals; some of the carved wood human caricatures would fit nicely into little Clara's dream and Tchaikovsky's *Nutcracker Suite.*

Key to Illustrations

Fig 1: Carved in fine detail, possibly in France or what was once known as French Indo-China, this picturesque old Buddhist monk is made of light mahogany. There is a recess in the back of the head where the nuts are cracked. **Fig. 2:** This boldly carved nutcracker from Russia represents a mustached and bewhiskered peasant wearing a snug round cap known as an astrakhan. Every feature is meticulously carved; the pupils of the eyes are black beads. **Fig. 3:** This screw-type nutcracker, 7" high, topped by a handsome pewter bust of Christopher Columbus, is a souvenir of the World's Columbian Exposition held in Chicago in 1893. **Fig. 4:** Dainty little screw-type nutcracker from the Chamonix Valley, France. A beautiful example of the work of French woodcarvers of the middle to late 18th century. This delicately carved head of a girl with bacchanalian features

11

and wearing a stylized Liberty Cap of the French revolutionary period is of cherry wood and stands 6" high. Nuts are placed in a receptacle in back of the head and crushed by turning the threaded handle. **Fig. 5:** This husky German hausfrau's sturdy jaws crack nuts with ease. It is a fine example of Black Forest woodcarving. **Fig. 6:** This walnut nutcracker, carved in Italy, is unique in that it represents two images of a Roman civilian dignitary. Both faces bear a striking resemblance to a one-time notorious Russian premier—whether intentional or not, we do not know. The long peaks of the Rome University hats serve as handles. **Fig. 7:** Cast iron squirrel nutcracker of American manufacture, ca. 1900; 4" high. **Fig. 8:** Carved of beechwood, this foot-high Schwartzwald hunter is of natural wood partially stained a dark brown. He has glass eyes and cracks nuts with his jaws. **Fig. 9:** Heavy brass nutcracker with grotesque masks. England, late 19th century. **Fig. 10:** Modern Italian-made nutcrackers of carved and painted wood. **Fig. 11:** Many breeds of dogs are represented in the woodcarvings made in Germany. This sad-eyed, flop-eared hound appears to represent a beagle.

Tramp Art

by *LESTER P. BREININGER, JR.*

Pencil box of various colored woods, edge-cut, and with hand carved knob on sliding lid. 8 inches long; 2 ½ inches high. Revi collection.

TRAMP ART, a name applied to numerous articles turned out by gentlemen of the leisure set, appears to have had its heyday between 1880 and 1914. Itinerants were most numerous and productive in these pre-World War I years. Among the items produced were animals in the round, bird trees, Noah in the Ark, Christmas yard animals and houses, wooden chains, handsome walking canes, and cigar box treasures. Such keepsakes were also turned out by prison inmates as well as by the hobo roamers of our countryside.

Tramps, literally "foot walkers,"

readily gathered discarded wooden cigar boxes, the basic ingredient of their craft; cigarette smoking was not then in vogue and cigar boxes were plentiful. Having acquired a supply, and time not being a factor of importance, the carver was ready to fabricate an item designed to catch a farmwife's fancy. This could then be peddled, or traded for food and lodging throughout the settlements. Tramp Art is found throughout Pennsylvania and New York and surrounding parts, including Canada.

The favorite item manufactured was the comb and brush holder. The parts,

Box with hearts on strap handle; painted brown. Length 9 inches; height 6 ½ inches. Cigar box wood under lid reads "Little Criterion." Privately owned.

Varnished trinket box, footed, with hinged cover. Secret compartment in top of box and interior of box lined with red satin. Height 5 ½ inches. Collection Mrs. Frank Moffitt.

being cut out of cigar box wood—often stamped with cigar advertising—were fastened together with small nails and/or glue. Usually a good sharp pocket knife was the only tool employed. Often the piece was embellished with notches cut from the board ends. This chip carving, or edge carving, resulted in maximum decoration with minimum tool requirements.

Comb boxes were either hung on the back porch for use when the men washed up for dinner, or were used to decorate the bedroom. The author

The raw material for Tramp Art usually consisted of old cigar boxes of the type shown above.

Hanging comb case dated 1922. Carved hearts, bell, leaves, acorns, horse's head, barrel, glass, bottle. Heavily varnished. Height 24 inches. Privately owned.

Jewelry chest with two drawers and lift-top compartment. The graceful curves of the Empire-style legs seem strangely compatible with the heavy edge-carved pyramidal decoration. Height 7 ¾ inches. Collection Mrs. D. M. Robl.

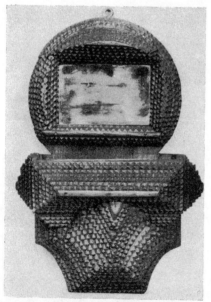

Hanging comb case with mirror. Back board from box imprinted "Di Girogio/Fruit Corporation." Height 16 inches. Collection Marcia Ray.

knows of several such holders still on the walls of the now enclosed back porches of farm folk who got them directly from the makers.

Further elaboration of the edge carving technique was achieved by using six to ten layers of cigar box wood, each succeeding one smaller than the last, to build up the desired pyramid effect. This form of decoration was used most often on picture frames and jewelry boxes. Critics of this style of embellishment often refer to it as "late attic" or "early monster."

The size of cigar boxes tended to control the dimensions of the finished articles, although careful jointing occasionally produced striking results. Less frequently, packing boxes of various sorts were used.

Match safes, newspaper holders, doll furniture, and trinket boxes also evolved from those old cigar boxes, and these, too, are now desirable items to collect. Tramp Art is only now be-

Picture frame with carved pyramidal decoration constructed of 10 layers of cigar box wood; dated 1898. Height 18 inches.

coming collectible and can still be obtained at reasonable prices. These objects are among the last remnants of American folk art still more or less available to the average collector.

Signed, dated specimens exist and may enable the collector to learn about the maker by inquiring of oldsters in the community. Unfortunately, some pieces have fake signatures, and this factor often leads to misinformation.

After the turn of the century, acorns and black walnut shell slices were used for quick and easy decorations. These embellishments usually gave a less desirable effect. With the diminishing supply of wooden cigar boxes and the rush of the modern age, Tramp Art faced extinction.

Folk Art in Miniature

by FRANK W. SAHULKA

Woodcock by Russell Burr, Hingham, Mass., 3¹/₄" long.

COMES A TIME the shelves you've built for your collection of decoys are filled—it doesn't take long if you acquire many as large as Lincoln slat geese—and you begin storing your surplus in boxes and barrels. Common sense says it's time to call a halt to collecting. But can you?

If you're like most collectors, the answer is "no". The urge to acquire is as strong as ever, and always present. To weed out or part with any portion of a collection is, if not unthinkable, extremely painful. Even Mr. Jack Barber in his *Wild Fowl Decoys* confesses himself "victimized by decoys".

Paperweights by Frank Adams, West Tisbury, Mass.; largest 10¹/₂", smallest 4". Paper label on bottom reads Frank Adams/ Maker of Marine Weathervanes/ West Tisbury, Mass.

Shooting gallery birds and animals; top bird is in cast clay, other in cast iron.

Dovecote or birdhouse carvings, three with late paint removed to show original color, secured in South Jersey, and belived to have been made there.

Bird carvings by gifted amateurs: two at left, found in Baltimore, Md. are attributed to a Baltimore carver. The redwing, right, was found in New York State, origin and maker unknown.

What is the answer? Do we stop, or do we go on buying and storing away?

Perhaps the solution lies in another direction—the miniature!

Many of the more talented of the decoy makers carved and painted, to scale, miniatures of the game birds they knew so well. These small ducks, geese, grouse, woodcock, and such are fairly literal copies of the birds they represent.

Of the old carvers, Elmer Crowell and his son Cleon of East Harwich, Massachusetts, and Joseph W. Lincoln of Accord, Massachusetts, are perhaps the best known. The Crowells made their miniatures in two sizes, $1/4$ and $1/8$ scale, and impressed their stamp in the bottom of the base. Lincoln's birds were usually not marked, but can be identified by the fine life-like quality of the painting.

Frank Adams of West Tisbury, Massachusetts, on Martha's Vineyard, was best known for his marine weathervanes, but he also carved working decoys and some wonderfully painted and finished game bird paperweights. In general, the miniature carvers followed the tradition of their trade and gave their birds the flat finish of the working decoy. Adams, however, finished his paperweight miniatures in a smooth high gloss.

The first Adams paperweight I came across was a female Mallard, $10^{1}/2$ inches long. I could get no information about it other than that it was a paperweight. About four years later I found four more duck paperweights obviously from the same hand. To my delight, each one of these bore the paper sticker label of Frank Adams on the bottom.

Canada Goose and Female Wood Duck, by Elmer Crowell, East Harwich, Mass.; wood duck 4⁵/₈" long, goose 6" long; impressed label on bottom reads: A. E. Crowell/ Maker/ East Harwich, Mass.

On making inquiries of the Town Clerk of West Tisbury, I was told that Mr. Adams had made weathervanes and decoys and paperweights on the Vineyard for many years and had passed away in 1944.

Though I have never seen another Adams paperweight since, many must be tucked away in the family desks of New England.

There were other miniature makers, examples of whose work are just beginning to be appreciated and identified.

One is Russel Burr, of Hingham, Massachusetts, who came from a family of bucket and firkin makers, and who also made working decoys. His beautiful little woodcock, just 3¼ inches from tail to bill tip is pictured here.

There has been much speculation about the origin of these miniatures. Why did these gunner craftsmen, whose hand was trained to the hatchet, draw knife and rasp turn to the finer tools necessary in the making of these delicate little cupboard pieces. They were certainly not made as samples, as they

in no way resemble decoys. The most likely theory advanced to date is that they were first made as gifts and toys for children.

There are also charming iron and clay shooting gallery birds and animals. Although often rough cast and chunky, they have the balance and simplicity of all true folk art, and show the same simplicity and utilitarian purity of design that is so evident in the working decoy.

In the same category are the carvings of the gifted amateur. Do you remember the dovecotes and birdhouses that were on the sides of barns? What became of the carved birds that sometimes decorated them? A few that merit interest as folk art are pictured here. When found, they were covered with a heavy coat of yellow paint. Careful removal exposed the original paint rather crudely applied. They, also, have the simple charm that makes the work of the amateur artist so much a part of the American scene.

Miniatures were *my* answer to overcrowded decoy shelves. Now the shelves that were made to house the miniatures are overflowing! What next?

Tiffany Metalware Productions

by HOWARD J. LOCKWOOD

THE WOULD BE COLLECTOR, fascinated by Tiffany but disheartened by the rising prices of desirable Tiffany glass, will find, relatively untouched by collectors, the metalware articles produced by Tiffany Studios. Tiffany Studios made not only the bronze bases for the Tiffany lamps, but also candlesticks, figurines, enamelled bronze pieces, tableware, desk sets, and an abundance of other useful and decorative objects.

Tiffany Studios was an outgrowth of the Tiffany Glass and Decorating Company which started producing and selling Tiffany lamps in 1895, stamping the bases with the monogram TG&DCo.

Reticulated glass candlestick; opaque jade-green glass and "Tiffany Green" bronze; marked "Tiffany Studios — New York"; height 14¾".

Left: Gold finished Chinese Pattern ashtray with match holder, 6¾ x 3¾". Right: Gold finished planter with copper insert, 8 x 3½". Author's collection.

After the lamps became popular, Tiffany designed candlesticks and candlelamps and production started in the late 1890s. These were also stamped with the TG&DCo monogram. In 1900, the name of the Tiffany Glass and Decorating Company was changed to Tiffany Studios, and thereafter all pieces were so stamped.

Tiffany Studios made use of four finishes on their bronze pieces. The most famous is the gold bronze which is recognizable by its yellow finish. The brown patina finish can be recognized by its smooth, brown finish. The gold finish was used on some desk sets and can be distinguished from the gold bronze finish in that it's more realistic gold in color. The most popular finish is the dark green finish used on many candlesticks and lamp bases.

DESK SETS

In starting a collection of articles produced by Tiffany Studios, one should decide on a definite area of concentration. Next to the lamps and candlesticks, probably the best known Tiffany Studios articles are the desk sets. Assembling a desk set is the easiest and least expensive way to start a collection of Tiffany bronzes. All one needs initially are two

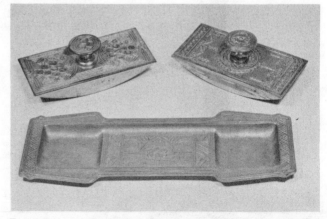

Top, left and right: Abalone Pattern and Adams Pattern gold finished rocking blotters; both 5½ x 2¾". Bottom: Gold finished American Indian Pattern pen tray, 11 x 4". Author's collection.

blotter ends and an inkwell. From then a collection of various items can be assembled. Of the approximately 35 items to choose from, the following are most popular: envelope openers, rocking blotters, letter racks, pen trays, clocks, paper clips, magnifying glasses, lamps, and candlesticks.

Tiffany Studios produced these sets in many different patterns, but three —the Zodiac, the Grape Vine, and the Pine Bough—stand out for popularity and availability.

The Pine Bough design, the first desk set pattern, appeared in 1900. The Grape Vine pattern followed. By 1909, the Zodiac, Bookmark, Ninth Century, Venetian, and Byzantine patterns were in production. The Abalone, Chinese, and American Indian patterns were introduced later. Most of the Tiffany Studios bronze articles were in production by 1919. All of the pieces were stamped "Tiffany Studios, New York," with an accompanying stock number.

Perhaps the easiest pattern for the beginner to recognize is the Zodiac, with the signs of the Zodiac deeply impressed into the bronze. Occasionally the signs of the Zodiac were polychromed (colored) on some of the pieces. Four finishes were used in the manufacture of this desk set: the gold bronze, the brown patina, the green and the silver-gold.

A great number of Zodiac pattern accessories are available, including a magnifying glass, a choice of three lamps, and candlesticks. One of the lamps available is similar in shape to that pictured in Revi's *American Art Nouveau Glass,* figure 132, except the Zodiac lamp usually has a white leaded shade and Zodiac signs are impressed around the base. The second Zodiac lamp has a narrow 1-inch bronze shade with the Zodiac signs impressed on the shade. The most desirable lamp is the common Turtleback lamp with the Zodiac signs impressed around the shade and base.

According to the 1915 Tiffany Catalogue the two most popular desk sets—Pine Bough and Grape Vine —were produced in two finishes, the brown and the gold. Another catalog stated that they were available in "green" and "gold" finish. The green and brown finished pieces are usually set with mottled green and white glass as a background for the cut-out areas of the background, whereas the gold finish has a caramel and white colored glass as an insert. There are variations to this, some have a blue glass background. Blotter ends, though they have the cut-out patterns, did not have the glass background. As with the Zodiac pattern, lamps and candlesticks are available. Take care when buying these patterns: First, because the glass is frequently cracked after fifty years of use, and second since the Revere Studios, a rival of Tiffany's, produced a pattern similar to the Grape Vine, such pieces are often found mixed in with Tiffany pieces, even though they are stamped Revere Studios.

The other desk sets made by Tiffany Studios tend to be more elaborate, very handsome pieces, and are much in demand. The Abalone set is always in the gold finish. These pieces are extremely attractive with groupings of either three or eight roundels of iridescent Abalone shell inlaid in the design. The selection of pieces available in this pattern was almost as great as that of the Zodiac pattern. Although Tiffany didn't keep records of his output, it may be assumed that this set and the others we have mentioned, were a limited production when compared to the Grape Vine, Pine Bough, or the Zodiac patterns.

The Ninth Century pattern is as attractive as the Abalone. Pieces in this set can be easily identified by the jade green colored glass used throughout their gold finish. Back in 1915 this desk set, by the piece, sold for twice as much as the Zodiac pattern. In fact, the Ninth Century lamp sold for $175 as compared to $45 for the Zodiac lamp. Tiffany also made special order pieces for this particular pattern.

The American Indian pattern is geometrical in design with raised Indian heads. This set comes in the brown patina and in the bronze dore finish, and is always signed, though not always numbered. Occasionally, these pieces are polychromed.

The Bookmark pattern was produced in the gold finish. It consists of sculptured birds, trees, and flowers impressed in individual squares. Like the Zodiac pattern, once seen, it is easily recognized.

INKWELLS

Tiffany inkwells, which were made on a limited scale apart from the desk sets, were very popular, and are now highly desirable. In many of these, Tiffany Studios used different colored glasses, the most common color being jade green. The procedure, identical to the candlesticks, was to form the bronze base with openings to accommodate the glass. The glass was then blown out from the inside so that it protruded through the bronze. These pieces are called "reticulated," and many inkwells were produced using this technique. A most unusual one is shaped like a crab. Tiffany relied heavily on the sea for many of his designs, so it is not surprising to find an inkwell in this form.

FIGURINES

Tiffany Studios also produced bronze figurines. Among the most popular are the bronze bulldog and the owl, both of which are quite lifelike. Tiffany also took the opportunity to indulge his sense of humor with figurines of droll little people. Sphinxs and lions were also popular. All of the figures are signed "Tiffany Studios" and show great exactness and detail.

TABLEWARE

Tiffany Studios seemed to produce every useful item that would sell. I have seen elaborate teapots, signed not "Tiffany and Co." but "Tiffany Stu-

dios." Tiffany Studios made many plates ranging in size from 5 inches to large trays with roundels of Abalone shell inserted into the rim. Most of the plates had a geometric design impressed around the rim. The popular Greek Key design was used extensively. Tiffany Studios also made compotes to match these plates. Some of these were finished in 14-karat gold plate with the householder's initials inscribed in the center. Also produced were many vases, some in the popular trumpet shape. These generally had a bronze dore finish with enamelling around the base. The enamelling usually appears as a subdued blend of colors; such pieces are highly desirable today. They have the usual Tiffany imprint and number with the word "Favrile" added.

ASH STANDS

For the smoker, Tiffany Studios supplied a wide variety of floor ash stands. These were made in the bronze dore finish and in the brown patina finish. Some are adjustable in height, while others remain stationary. Some of the ash stand bases are done in the same pattern as that used for lamp

Tiffany Studio pen trays. **Top to bottom: Gold finished Modelled Pattern, 9 x 3". Silver-gold finished Zodiac Pattern, 10 x 3". Gold finished Bookmark Pattern, 8¾ x 2¾". Author's collection.**

bases, such as a tree trunk, while others are plain in design. Many were fitted with removable Favrile glass bowls.

Double picture frame of gold finished metal in the Vineyard pattern with mottle green and white glass background; marked "Tiffany Studios — New York"; height 6½".

CANDLESTICKS

The two most frequently encountered of Tiffany Studios' many candlesticks, are those with the plain bobeche and those with jade green glass protruding through the reticulated bronze. Candlesticks with the plain bronze bobeche generally have the bobeche resting on three arms. The reticulated bobeche is usually screwed directly into the candlestick stem. The stems were straight and between 12 and 20 inches in height. Other bases included two-arm candlesticks, and candlesticks shaped like a serpent supporting the bobeche. Tiffany Studios' output of candlesticks was tremendous, so one can form an endless collection of these.

There are many other examples of Tiffany Studios' metalware productions. It is best for the collector to choose one area of concentration at a time, lest he find himself overextended.

"Mountain Goat Bookends," by Anna Hyatt Huntington; 7½" high; base 5½" by 8". Finished in light brown patine ($135).

Gorham's Small Bronzes

by MARCIA RAY

"Appeal to the Great Spirit," by Cyrus Dallin. Reproduced in various heights: 9¾" ($100); 21¾" ($350); and 36" ($1300). Finished in brown patine.

IN THOSE LUSH Tiffany days, from the 1890s to the 1930s when the Great Depression put an end to elegance, small objets d'art, bronzes among them, were in high favor.

This turn of the century period, when America had arrived at a position of power and independence in world affairs and had, at last, time for the refinements of life, was marked by a growth of characteristic national art. American artists, educated in American schools, turned to subjects distinctly American in character—Indians, the Wild West, animals, athletic sports, children—and their techniques reflected the national spirit of sturdy simplicity.

Small bronzes were an effective medium for the expression of this spirit. In small sculpture, few incidentals can be brought into the composition. The figure itself must express in its pose and technique, with simplicity, beauty, and sincerity, what the sculptor has in mind. Even the most important sculptors of the day rose to the challenge, and their small bronzes made the finest of American sculpture available to homes of moderate means across the country.

Some of these bronzes were reductions of well known statues by important contemporary artists, like Cyrus Dallin's "Appeal to the Great Spirit" which stands before the Museum of Fine Arts in Boston, Mass. Others were designed expressly for garden pieces and table ornaments.

They were never inexpensive. A Gorham Company's price list for 1929 shows prices ranging from $30 for a 2¹/₂ inch high "Conventional Elephant" by Margaret Postgate to $3,500 for a 7 ft. 4 in. fountain, "Glint of the Sea," by Chester Beach. (The same subject, 7⁵/₈ inches high, was $85.)

While Gorham was not the only company to manufacture small bronzes, it was undoubtedly the most prestigious of American makers. The sculptures they presented were done by renowned artists; materials and workmanship used in reproduction were of highest quality.

In 1929, to promote this facet of their production, the Gorham Company of New York (the company's retail division) published a handsome hard-bound catalog called *Famous Small Bronzes*, subtitled on its title page, "A represen-

"Flying Sphere," by R. Tait McKenzie; 22½" high, mounted on black and gold pencil-point marble. Suitable as a trophy for athletic events or as a decorative bronze for home or club ($500).

"Speed," by Harriet W. Frishmuth, silver electro-plated over bronze for decorating raditor caps of fine automobiles, came in two sizes, 4" high by 8" long ($80) and 6" by 12" ($125). Also suitable as a trophy for athletic events.

"Bronco Buster," by Frank E. Dodge. 17¾" high; finished in mottled green patine ($295).

tative Exhibit selected from the works of noted contemporary sculptors." It contained 48 full-page sepia-finished photographic illustrations with separating tissues on which was printed a description of the subject; two pages of biographical notes on the sculptors represented; and a loose supplement of prices. The small bronzes pictured were at that time on exhibition—and for sale—at the Gorham Galleries at 5th Avenue and 47th Street, New York.

The Gorham Company has a long history. James Gorham, a goldsmith in Providence, R.I., began making jewelry and other small items in 1815. In 1831, as Gorham & Webster, he added silver spoons. Through the years, as silver-

smiths of high quality, the Gorham name persisted—as Gorham, Webster & Price, 1837-1841; J. Gorham & Son, 1841-1850; Gorham & Thurber, 1850-1852; Gorham & Company, 1852-1865; Gorham Mfg. Company, 1865-1961. In 1961, it became the Gorham Corp. which it is today.

The Bronze Division was added in 1885 when ecclesiastic wares of gold, bronze, stone, wood and sterling became part of the Gorham production.

The Gorham Galleries where the small bronzes were displayed and sold was the company's New York retail store. In 1929, it merged with Black, Starr and Frost to become Black, Starr and Frost-Gorham, Inc. at the same address. In 1940 the name was shortened to Black, Starr & Gorham, Inc. Then in 1962, the Gorham Company sold its interests and the store reverted to Black, Starr & Frost, Ltd.

The Depression, so close at hand when *Famous Small Bronzes* appeared in 1929, curtailed immediate sales of such luxuries. Then came World War II with its aftermath of family movement, smaller houses, and changes in decorative as well as life styles. Today more and more of these small bronzes are appearing in antiques shops, and collectors and dealers alike are puzzling over the signatures on their bases. Some of the artists' names are well known; others require research.

The "Biographical Notes" given in Gorham's *Famous Small Bronzes* on those sculptors whose work was pictured in the catalog were current in 1929. Though they contained the artist's birthplace—perhaps to stress American origin and encourage regional pride—no birth dates were given.

These "Notes," with the omission of schools attended, honors received, and societies to which the artists belonged, are given below. It seems enough to know where these sculptors were born, something of their specialties, the museums in which their work was represented, and may still be seen, the cities in which their monuments stand and, particularly, that they made small bronzes for Gorham.

Angela, Emilio—Born in Italy. Studied sculpture at Cooper Union, architecture at Columbia University. Created garden pieces "for various estates, the best known on the estate of Joseph P. Day."

Beach, Chester—Born, San Francisco, Calif. Represented in the Cleveland Museum; Brooklyn Museum; Art Institute of Chicago; St. Mark's Church, N. Y.; Hall of Fame, N. Y.

Borglum, Gutzon—Born in Idaho. Represented by many monuments, best known of which are his Lincoln Head, Washington, D.C.; seated Lincoln, Newark, N.J.; The Flyer, Univ. of Va. Several smaller bronzes in the Metropolitan Museum of Art.

Clark, Allen—Born, Missoula, Montana. Represented in the Fogg Museum, Cambridge, Mass.; Metropolitan Museum; Museum of Honolulu; Univ. of Washington. Many of his important bronzes privately owned.

Conkling, Mabel—Born, Boothbay, Maine. Represented in the Chicago Art Institute; Plastic Club, Phila. Specialty: Portrait and Garden Sculptures.

Dallin, Cyrus—Born, Springfield, Utah. Important monuments in many American cities, the best known: Signal of Peace, Chicago; Pioneer Monument, Salt Lake City; Medicine Man, Phila.; Appeal to the Great Spirit, Boston; The Scout, Kansas City; Massasoit, Plymouth, Mass. Also represented in the Boston Museum of Fine Arts and

"Pensive Scotty," by Marguerite Kirmse. 1½" high ($10).

Library of Congress, Washington, D.C.

Dodge, Frank E.—of Providence, R.I. An illustrator of note and formerly on the faculty of the R. I. School of Design. He produced several interesting pieces of sculpture, the most attractive, his "Broncho Buster."

Eberle, Abastenia St. Leger—Born, Webster City, Iowa. Represented in the Metropolitan Museum; Worcester (Mass.) Art Museum; Peabody Art Institute, Baltimore; Newark Museum; Chicago Art Institute; Carnegie Institute, Pittsburgh; Detroit Institute; Toledo Art Museum.

Fraser, Laura Gardin—Born, Chicago, Ill. "Many of her small bronzes can be found in prominent homes."

Frishmuth, Harriet—Born, Philadelphia. Represented in the Metropolitan Museum of Art; Museum of Fine Arts, Dayton; John Herron Art Institute, Indianapolis; Museum of Fine Arts, Houston; Museums in Dallas, Atlanta, and Los Angeles. "Many of her large fountains are placed on prominent estates and in private gardens."

Fuchs, Emil—Born, Vienna, Austria. Represented in the Metropolitan Museum; Cleveland Museum; British Museum; Victoria & Albert Museum, London. Memorials at Sandringham and Balmoral, also Ashley Memorial Rumsey Cathedral.

Gruppe, Karl—Born, Rochester, N.Y. Created models for the Panama Pacific Exposition, San Francisco, 1915, and the Sesqui-Centennial Exposition, Phila., 1926. Represented in City Club, New York; Princeton Charter Club.

Huntington, Anna Hyatt—Born, Cambridge, Mass. Represented in Metropolitan Museum; Cathedral St. John the Divine, N. Y. Monuments of Joan d'Arc in N. Y. City, Gloucester, Mass., Glois, France.

Jewett, Maude S.—Born, Englewood, N. J. Represented in the Cleveland Art Museum.

Johnson, Bernard P.—Born, Providence, R. I. Painter, Sculptor, Etcher. Executed numerous pieces of Memorial Sculpture besides many studies of animals.

Konti, Isidore—Born, Vienna, Aus-

"Bear and Rabbit" group signed and dated by the artist, "A. Phimister Proctor, '94." Copyrighted by Gorham Founders in 1895. 4⅛" high; dark brown patine. *Collection Mr. & Mrs. Hovey Gleason.*

tria. Came to the U. S. in 1890. Represented in the Metropolitan Museum; Detroit Institute; Minneapolis Institute; National Museum of Art, Washington, D.C.; St. Louis Museum. Monuments in Washington, Cleveland, New Orleans, Yonkers, Philadelphia and New York.

McKenzie, Robert Tait—Born, Almonte, Ontario, Canada. Represented in many important museums and Art Galleries, such as Fitz William Museum, Cambridge, England; Ashmolean Museum, Oxford; Metropolitan Museum; Canadian National Gallery; Art Gallery, Montreal; Brown Univ.; Univ. of Penn.; Newark Museum; St. Louis Art Museum. Monuments: Univ. of Penn., Phila.; Cambridge, England; Parliament Building, Ottawa, Canada; Princeton, N. J.; Edinburgh, Scotland. (In 1929 when these notes were compiled, he was Director of the Dept. of Physical

Education, Univ. of Penn.)

MacLeary, Bonnie—Born, San Antonio, Texas. Represented in the Metropolitan Museum and Children's Museum, Brooklyn, N. Y. Munos Rivera Monument, Puerto Rico; World War Memorial, San Juan, Puerto Rico. Numerous important garden subjects.

Parsons, Edith Barretto—Born, Houston, Va. Represented in the Metropolitan Museum of Art. Monuments in Memphis and St. Paul. Figure at Liberal Arts Building, St. Louis. "Her fountain figures of children will be found in many of the most important gardens."

Postgate, Margaret J.—Born, Chicago, Ill. Among her awards was the Beaux Art Medal in 1924 for Mural Painting.

Proctor, Alexander Phimister-Born, Bozanquit, Ontario. Specialty, Western subjects. Represented in Metropolitan and other important museums. Some of his most prominent

"Pinehurst (Caddy) Sundial," by Lucy Richards. 17½" tall; finished in brown patine ($325).

monuments: Puma Entrance to Prospect Park, Brooklyn, N.Y.; Tigers at Princeton Univ.; Buffaloes at Q Street Bridge, Washington, D.C.; Pioneer, Univ. of Oregon; Moose, Carnegie Institute, Pittsburgh; Equestrian of Roosevelt, Portland, Ore.; Broncho Buster, Denver; Indian Fountain, Lake George, N.Y.

Richards, Lucy C.—Born, Lawrence, Mass. Created decorative garden sculpture among which is the "Caddy" Sundial at Pinehurst, N. C.

Sears, Philip S.—Born, Boston, Mass. Member of the Guild of Boston Artists; North Shore Art Association; City Art Commission, Boston.

Yates, Julie Nicholls—Born, St. Louis, Mo. Exhibited in many of the most prominent Exhibitions including the Paris Salon. Specialty: Portraits and Garden Figures.

Young, Mahonri M.—Born, Salt Lake City, Utah. Represented in the Metropolitan Museum; American Museum of Natural History, N. Y.; Newark Museum; Peabody Institute, Baltimore, Md. Monument at Salt Lake City.

Among other sculptors whose Gorham-cast small bronzes were extremely popular, but were not included in the 1929 catalog, are:

Hughlette Wheeler, whose small bronze Westerns included "Loosened-up," "Let-er-Buck," "Ride'm Cowboy," and "The Mix-up" (horses and a steer);

J. Clinton Shepherd, who sculpted "The Horse Wrangler" (rider on horse and three wild horses) and "The Night Herd";

F. A. Williams, whose "Indian Arrow-maker" Sundial, 24 inches high, 30 inches long, sold for $600; and

Marguerite Kirmse, English-born artist, best known for her etchings of dogs. Her very small sculptures of Scotties (1½ to 2 inches high) which Gorham cast, sold for $10; her 8-inch Scotty bookends, for $90. She had become an American citizen and was then living at her farm, "Arcady," in Connecticut where she raised her own models—the Scotties, Irish Terriers, and Airedales, so popular in the 1920s and 1930s.

Pewter Ice Cream Molds in Table or Centerpiece Size

by DUNCAN B. WOLCOTT

ICE CREAM HAS been made commercially in the United States since 1786 when a Mr. Hall in New York began advertising his product, and molds for fashioning it into fancy shapes were mentioned as early as 1788 in the inventory of William Will, the Philadelphia pewterer. The earliest molds were used in the home or by private caterers. Not until the mid-19th century, when ice cream factories appeared, was molded ice cream packed commercially. Once on the market, molded ice cream enjoyed tremendous popularity among Victorian hostesses.

The pewter molds for making fancy ice cream desserts came in various sizes; "bite" size, to be assembled, as flowers or fruits in a basket; individual size, holding one-fourth pint; medium large, a table or centerpiece size to serve four to eight persons; and the large centerpiece size, a dramatic presentation to enliven a dinner party of 12 or more. A giant Statue of Liberty mold held 36 pints of ice cream, enough for a banquet.

Like the smaller molds, the centerpiece extravaganzas were made in a multitude of stock shapes to suit almost any occasion. They could also be custom-made, in his own design—at extra cost—for the determined individualist.

The two fundamental requirements for making quality molds—artistic ability and experienced craftsmanship —have always been constant. The sculptor must create the original image in such a form as to insure the making of a metal mold which will produce an artistic ice cream replica. The craftsman must be skilled to do the delicate chas-ing on the master metal mold in order to hold the lines of the original image. The large molds made in America were frequently, but not always, copies of European examples.

One of the last companies making ice cream molds today is Fr. Krauss' Son of Milford, Pa., a company established in 1860. In one of their wholesale catalogs issued in the 1930s, they offered 36 designs in the table or centerpiece size, a 5½ pint Musk Melon and a 5-pint Lobster being the largest. Also shown were the usual Heart for Valentine's Day, Santa for Christmas, Duck, Rabbit, and Lamb for Easter. Among off-beat molds for any day at all were a St. Bernard dog and a Lady on a Bicycle.

For all their variations, such late molds cannot compare in number of designs, weight of pewter, and overall intricacy with the molds available in the 19th and early 20th centuries when elaborate entertaining was at its peak and a towering ice cream centerpiece was appropriate.

Made in U.S.A.

Schall & Co., founded in New York in 1854, probably the oldest of American firms to make pewter ice cream molds, stamped their molds "S & Co." Eppelsheimer & Co., also of New York, and without question the largest producer of molds in this country, was founded in the early 1880s by Peter R. and Henry Eppelsheimer. They used the mark "'E

& Co. N Y." Their earliest dated molds were marked 1888. J. Ernst was another mold maker whose stamp "J. Ernst N. Y." is found on pewter ice cream molds. In Philadelphia, T. Mills & Bro., and Valentine Clad & Sons were active mold makers. There were dozens of lesser-known companies across the country engaged in this manufacture.

Many of the America-made large molds were copies of European examples, but both Schall and Eppelsheimer, at least, designed and made some distinctively American subject molds. Most large molds carry a cast number; Schall & Co. used numbers from 1 to 100; six late Schall molds, all fruits and vegetables, carry numbers in the 200 and 400 series. Eppelsheimer, numbers from 1 to 200.

Locomotive, by Eppelsheimer & Co., stamped "E & Co N Y"; Santa Claus and Battleship Maine, by Schall & Co., marked "S & Co." All are in the large size.

Made in France

Cow centerpiece molds: left, by Cadot; right, by Letang; individual serving mold indicates their large size.

The two earliest French mold makers were Cadot et Cie., founded in 1826, and the "House of Letang," founded in 1832. Both were located in Paris. Cadot used the trademark "C.C.," together with a cast mark representing an early hand-cranked ice cream freezer. Letang, which operated under various names over the years, used a stamped oval trademark and the cast letters "L. G.," representing the first and last letters in Letang.

Cadot centerpiece molds: French Locomotive, ca. 1850; Spaniel; and Basket of Flowers; shown with locomotive in individual size for size comparison.

Asparagus mold
with C. C. mark.

Cadot et Cie. Trademark

Letang trademark

Made in Germany

The largest producer of German molds was Johannes Reinöhl. He was born in Ulm in 1821, and used his home city, where his factory was located, in his trademark stamp. The important difference between his molds and those made elsewhere lay in the hinge con-struction. The Reinöhl-type hinge is made from thin strips of metal folded into loops and soldered to the mold. When a mold is found without its base plate and is therefore unmarked, it can be tentatively identified as to origin by the type of hinge.

Reinöhl centerpiece molds: Columbia, sometimes called Miss Liberty or Liberty (not to be confused with the Statue of Liberty mold); Eagle, one of the rarest of molds; and Horn of Plenty; shown with their individual serving size counterparts.

Gazebo and Lighthouse, marked only with stamped numbers, are typical of continental Europe; hinges and strap handles indicate either French or German manufacture.

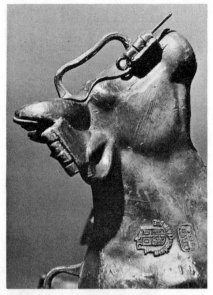

Mermaid, Dolphin, and Fish molds made by Reinöhl; Reinöhl hinges can be seen clearly on the Mermaid and the Dolphin.

Hinge commonly used on French, English, and American molds.

← Trademark of Johannes Reinöhl, Ulm, Germany

Made in England

As a general rule, English-made molds of the table or centerpiece variety fall into the medium large classification; some may hold only a pint of ice cream. When an English registry mark appears on the mold, it is easy to determine the exact date when the design was registered. Tables for registry marks can be found in almost any book on British pottery and porcelain. Since designs were used for many years, it is not possible to know the exact age of the mold itself, only how old it could be.

From their registry stamp, Biertumpfel and Hepting is shown to be working in England in 1868. More is known of Harton and Son, London. This firm was the successor to the early 19th-century London firm of Harton and Watts, Pewterers. In 1878, Harton and Son was located at 159 High Holbern St., W. C.,

Mark used by Harton and Son, London.

London, where they had moved from 61 Shoelane. They went out of business sometime before 1891.

Mark used by
Biertumpfel and
Hepting, London.

Sheaf of Wheat, design registered by Biertumpfel and Hepting, July 22, 1868; Fancy
Design, no maker's mark, stamped only with "7" and PINT; Pineapple (3-part mold) by
Harton and Son, London, design registered May 15, 1876. Individual size molds in identi-
cal designs indicate the medium size of the English table molds as compared with the
German large size.

Tin Advertising Trays

by ART and JEWEL UMBERGER

Change tray advertising the non-intoxicating "Lily, A Beverage," bottled only by Rock Island Brewing Co., Rock Island, Ill.; made by American Art Works, Coshocton, O.

Tray entitled "St. Louis Levee in Early Seventies" advertised Budweiser King of Bottled Beer, 1914; made by American Can Co., Chicago.

FAST MOVING into the field of popular collectibles are tin advertising trays and signs of comparatively recent vintage – the beer, whiskey, mineral water, and soda water trays of the 1890s to the 1930s. Trays advertising shoes, foodstuffs, patent medicines, and other articles are also becoming collectors' specialties. These tin pieces of Americana, once given away as souvenirs or premiums to promote products and goodwill simultaneously, are available today in antiques shops and shows.

Colorful trays comprise an interesting collection in themselves or add depth as related items for a bottle collection. Coca Cola trays will enrich

Coca Cola memorabilia, and Moxie trays or signs will enhance a collection of Moxie bottles. Both drinks were originally advertised as brain and nerve foods.

Serving trays were rectangular, round, or oval. The largest were 16 inches or more in diameter and were wall pieces or plaques used for decoration. The next smaller size, 12 to 16 inches, was probably most common. Tin art plates were 10 inches in diameter, and the miniature or "tip" size was about 4 inches. The small oval trays were approximately 4 x 6 inches.

The large trays or plaques such as Velvet Beer or Falstaff Beer are scarcer than the regular size trays. The picturesque scenes used on them add flavor to a collection and may be displayed to great advantage, although adequate space must be provided for them.

Budweiser Beer tray, "Say When," 1915-20; maker unknown.

The round art plates resemble porcelain when viewed at a distance. On these plates the name of the advertiser usually appeared on the reverse; the date "1905" is frequently seen on the back, also. Anheuser-Busch, Western Coca Cola, and others used this medium in advertising. In a baroque frame the art plate with its decorative border makes an elegant wall piece.

Few trays suggest their use, but one miniature tray, put out by the Dallas Brewing Company in 1908, bore the

word "Tip," printed in sizable letters.

Part of the fun of collecting trays is to trace the history of the firms who used them for advertising. The age of the trays is also exciting to a collector. Often the date is printed in an obscure corner, but it is not always this simple. It is difficult to date a tray until a number of them have been studied and examined. New trays may have old subjects. If a tray looks new and is not dated, it could be of recent issue.

A study of clothing and hair styles may help to approximate the age of a tray. Earlier trays (1900-1910) show women with flowing Grecian hair styles, while the flapper era is documented with short bobbed hair. Hat fashions, such as the 1914 bonnet of the "Betty" Coca Cola tray and the later cloche hats of the 1920s help date the tray. The picture hat of the girl on the 1917 Coke tray is another date setter.

Other characteristics aid in determining the age. For instance, in the 1920s most of the Coke trays had green and brown borders, while the 1930 trays had red borders.

A glass or bottle shown in a scene will sometimes indicate the date. Older Coke glasses were flared and imprinted with the 5 cent mark. Coke bottles of the 1890s had blob tops and Hutchinson stoppers; 1900-1915 bottles had straight sides; later bottles were skirted. Beer and whiskey bottles with cork-stoppered mouths were earlier

Wall plaque, "The Home of Fallstaff," made by Lemp, St. Louis, ca. 1905.

Left: Coca Cola tray, 1917, marked Stelad Signs, Passaic Metal Ware Co., Passaic, N.J. Above: Coca Cola Tray, 1925, by the American Art Works, Coshocton, O.

Portrait trays: left, Coca Cola, "Betty," 1914; top, Star Union Brewing Co.'s Pure Beers, Peru, Ill., 1905, maker unknown; right, Coca Cola, 1917; bottom, Coca Cola, 1912, artist-signed "Hamilton King." All Coca Cola trays here made by Passaic Metal Ware Co., Passaic, N.J.

than those with crown caps. Most early whiskey bottles were cylindrical; later bottles had fluted shoulders and base.

Manufacturers of early trays included: The Meek Company, American Art Works (successors to Meek Co.), and H. D. Beach Company, all of Coshocton, Ohio; Passaic Metalware Company of New Jersey; Kauffmann & Strauss of New York; Wolf & Company, Chas. W. Shonk of Chicago; and

Mayer & Lavenson of New York. In addition to the maker's name a tray may have the artist's signature on it, such as the 1912 tray of the Coca Cola Company which bears the signature of Hamilton King, a well-known artist of that day. Christian Feigenspan Brewing Company's tray of a lovely lady is signed "A. Asti." A signature will add value to a tray.

Stock designs could be obtained from manufacturers, and this economical factor helped small businesses to select a design and have their name stamped upon the trays at a nominal cost. Many different firms used the

Tray entitled "In Old Kentucky," artist-signed "Chs. J. Collins," advertised Stars and Stripes Bottled Beer, Willow Springs Brewing Co., Omaha, U.S.A., 1912; made by American Art Works, Coshocton, O.

same popular design. The larger firms used original designs.

How is the desirability of a tray determined? Pictures of a bygone era such as the 1914 Budweiser tray depicting a steamboat unloading on the Mississippi or the Prohibition trays with non-alcoholic beverages add importance to a collection. Trays with bitters advertising are a rare treat. The Lashes Bitters plaques and the Royal Pepsin Bitters tray are outstanding. The latter was silver-plated by the Homan Company between 1900-1922.

Tin pictures are more difficult to find than tin trays. Printed on a tin-

like material they were washable and fairly permanent. Subjects varied, but animals were popular. A Pickwick Ale piece, an elongated tin picture, shows two large horses pulling a dray on which is strapped three huge kegs of ale. The tin was manufactured by American Art Works and directions printed on the back state: "To keep this sign clean and bright wipe the surface of it every thirty days with a damp cloth." Another tin picture, for Hanley's Peerless Ale, has only the lettering and an enormous reclining bulldog. Some of the tin pictures were framed; others, with the raw edges turned under, had cardboard backs with corks for hanging.

Large framed pictures stamped from a single piece of tin are real prizes. They measure as large as 2 by 3 feet or more. The self-frame gives added depth to the picture. The marvelous tin picture of young Theodore Roosevelt returning from a hunt is a prime collector's item. Another picture, entitled "True Fruit," advertising a soda fountain drink, is a choice item. Small advertising trays are usually inexpensive, though some of the well-advertised Western Coca Cola "topless" beauties fetch fancy prices. The "Betty" calendar, shown here from an advertisement in a 1913 *Farm & Home* magazine, is now a collector's dream. Attention should be given to the

Tray advertising The Geo. T. Stagg Company, Inc., Frankfort, Ky., Makers of O.F.C. Bourbon, date unknown; made by Electrical Chemical Engraving Co., New York, N.Y.

condition of the tray. If the tray is just
as it came from the factory it may be
called "mint." With minor wear signs
on rim or tiny scratches, it may be
considered excellent or good, according to the degree of wear. Any' marks
or defacing of the subject matter are
undesirable.

These trays, although they are not
antique, represent the "good old
days," when children were always
rosy-cheeked and in robust health,
when a fashionably attired lady looked
every bit a lady, the essence of poise,
whether she held a glass or a bottle,
whether she was lightly draped or fully
clothed, and when gentlemen appeared
to glow with an inner satisfaction, re-
flecting the opulence of those splendid
days.

**Write for
"Betty"**

That's the name
of the beautiful
girl on the

Coca-Cola

*1914
Calendar*

(Size, 13 X 32 inches)

Send your name and
address and a 2c stamp
(it pays part of the
postage) and we'll
send you promptly
postpaid this beautifully lithographed and perfect reproduction of the oil painting
"Betty," painted especially for
us. 1914 calendar is attached.

FREE

Coca-Cola booklet on request
THE COCA-COLA CO.
Atlanta, Ga.

Advertisement in the magazine FARM AND
HOME, Dec. 1, 1913.

Reflections of Our Past

by DR. BURTON SPILLER

Fig. 1

Fig. 2

IN TODAY'S MAD, wonderful world of collecting, many items have become highly prized as collectibles that even a decade ago were considered unworthy of notice. The advertising pocket mirror is one of these, swept into importance

Fig. 3

Fig. 4

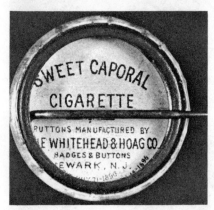

Fig. 5

ful while oval ones are considered most desirable.

In some mirrors the viewer can see only a small portion of his face—an eye, lips, or nose—depending on how the mirror is held. Other mirrors have a slightly convex surface and the viewer can readily see his entire face.

Pocket mirrors are seldom smaller than 1³/₄ inches in diameter nor larger than 2³/₄ inches. A collection of items this small can be colorful yet not occupy a great deal of space. While some larger advertising mirrors—3¹/₂ to 4 inches in diameter—called paperweight mirrors were made *(Fig. 2)*, the pocket types are most avidly collected.

Paperweight mirrors were often given by a parent company for use in branch managers' offices. They might commemorate a company anniversary or special occasion and were made in limited quantities. Pocket mirrors, on the other hand, were made in continual numbers to be given away to any man or woman who would "take the message home."

The materials used on the advertising side of these small mirrors were cel-

with the burgeoning interest in all early advertising material.

Any items to be collectible should have a common denominator which unites them. This factor makes the difference between just an accumulation of things and a true collection. The unifying factor with pocket mirrors is the mirror. It may be round, oval, or rectangular *(Fig. 1);* these are the three basic shapes. Round mirrors are most plenti-

luloid, paper, or metal *(Fig. 3)*. Celluloid is a hard plastic-like substance of pyroxylin (cellulose nitrates) and camphor, usually colorless or resembling ivory. Because an endless variety of colorful design was possible by using celluloid, advertising mirrors of that type are most usually found and collectors like them best. The graphics on some are truly superb *(Fig. 4)*.

Paper and metal backed mirrors lack advantages of design and color and rely primarily on words to promote products. While these were cheaper to make, most advertisers preferred· celluloid. Therefore, non-celluloid backed mirrors of any kind are scarcer though not as prized as celluloid ones.

Manufacturing advertising mirrors was similar to processes used in making advertising buttons. Design on earlier mirrors was applied to celluloid from lithographed stones, while printing presses did the printed parts. Photographic processes replaced lithography on later mirrors.

The celluloid was pressed over a shell and adhered to a metal ring or collet which also aided in keeping the mirror in place. In all, each mirror went through six steps before it was ready for shipment. It was blanked out on large

Fig. 6

Fig. 7

sheets, printed, formed, mirror inserted, inspected, and finally packed.

The majority of advertising pocket mirrors were made by three large companies specializing in novelty advertising: The Whitehead & Hoag Company, Newark, N.J.; Bastian Brothers Company, Rochester, N.Y.; and Parisian Novelty Company, Chicago, Ill. The most prolific maker of the three seems to have been Whitehead & Hoag, a company formed in 1892 by Benjamin S. Whitehead, owner of a Newark print shop, and Chester R. Hoag, a businessman.

In the 1890s celluloid came into gen-

Fig. 8

Fig. 9

Fig. 10

Fig. 11

eral use for novelty products, having made its way slowly from the time of its invention in 1869. The American Tobacco Company, accustomed to giving away cigarette pictures of popular American celebrities, conceived the idea of using celluloid buttons instead, one to each package of cigarettes. Whitehead & Hoag, familiar with the new substance, received the first big order. The pinback feature for attaching buttons was Mr. Whitehead's invention.

The success of these buttons (*Fig. 5*) was astonishing. Tobacco companies demanded them at the rate of 1 million a day; heavy reorders kept the button business moving. Products so advertised were innumerable. On the fun side, fashionable young sports began to appear with such sentiments as "If You Love Me, Grin," "Kiss Me Quick," and "You're Not The Only Pebble On The Beach" emblazoned in celluloid on their lapels.

Advertising mirrors were a variation on this button idea. Since mirrors had a practical function regardless of advertising, their useful life was substantially longer than that of buttons.

It is not unusual to find both a celluloid mirror and button showing the same scene and advertising. With pocket mirrors, as with their multitude of other advertising novelties, from calendars to letter openers to magnifying glasses, Whitehead & Hoag's own art staff was usually responsible for design. However, on occasional special orders notable artists and sculptors were employed. An eminent turn-of-the-century artist, Hamilton King, created the 1909 Coca-Cola girl. Her likeness can be found on Coke trays and paper advertising as well as mirrors. *(Fig. 6)*.

Bastian Brothers Company *(Fig. 7)* was founded in 1895 by Theron E. and Frederick J. Bastian. They began as retail jewelers in Rochester, N.Y. In 1906 they bought the Pulver Company, a local firm specializing in making chocolates and advertising items. (Pulver then went into the business of manufacturing gum, an enterprise which ended in 1954. Pulver Gum machines, once numerous, are now choice collectibles.)

Bastian Brothers grew rapidly, gaining leadership in the manufacture of buttons, mirrors, and political badges of every description plus all types of novelty advertising. In 1959 they acquired their largest competitor, Whitehead & Hoag Company, in a merger which has made Bastian the national leader in the field.

One of the most wanted early soft drink pocket mirrors depicts the Hires Root Beer girl *(Fig. 8)*, made by Bastian Brothers.

The Parisian Novelty Company began business in 1898 and is still actively engaged in producing advertising and plastic specialties. The company also makes presses, accessories, and parts for "do it yourself" button-making machinery and equipment. Their hand-operated presses *(Fig. 9)* can also be used for assembling pocket mirrors. Mirror reproductions as well as snapshots made into mirrors can be produced this way.

The mirror shown in *Fig. 10* is not an old one. It undoubtedly was made by laminating a Singer Sewing Machine Company trade card. Note how the woman's head has been cut off the right side of the mirror. No original mirror would exhibit so incomplete a design.

Pocket mirror manufacturers offered their customers both individual designs and stock designs upon which a slogan, trade mark, or other message could be printed. A mirror with a border of birthstones *(Fig. 11)* is the most commonly found stock design. The customer's message was printed in the center. Stock designs cost less than special

Fig. 14

et mirrors, the collector can readily spot a fake.

It isn't unusual to find more than one mirror design advertising the same product (*Fig. 14*). Almost a dozen different Coca-Cola pocket mirrors were distributed between 1904 and 1924. To own a complete set of original Coke mirrors is the pocket mirror collector's dream.

An elegant variation in pocket mirror design is the celluloid mirror with a graceful metal border ending in a fancy handle (*Fig. 15*). As giveaways these

Fig. 12   **Fig. 18**

Fig. 13

order designs which identified one product only (*Fig. 12*).

Most mirror manufacturers printed their names somewhere on the celluloid, usually around the border near its junction with the collet (*Fig. 13*). It can be seen when the mirror is viewed at a 45 degree angle. The maker's name is not visible on every old mirror, but when it is found, it is proof the mirror is original for no name would be seen on a reproduction mirror. With a little experience in observing and handling pocket mirrors, the collector can readily

were expensive for the advertiser, but must have made his product unforgettable to the consumer.

Most mirror designs were directed towards female approval as women did most of the family shopping. However, those mirrors aimed primarily at the man of the house are memorable (*Fig. 16*).

While design and graphics can make one mirror more desirable than another, subject matter is also important. Currently, mirrors concerning drinkable

Fig. 19

Fig. 16

Fig. 15

products, such as soft drinks, beer, whiskey, and patent medicines *(Fig. 17)*, are most favored. Many bottle collectors are discovering what great "go-withs" mirrors make for their bottles. Tobacco-related mirrors and those showing pretty girls are eagerly sought. One collector, at least, seeks only "good for" mirrors; that is, mirrors used as trade tokens with the amount of money they were good for in trade stated on them. *(Fig. 18)*.

Pocket mirrors came into vogue in the early 1900s and continued in popularity until the late 1930s, when the growth of radio broadcasting and a surge of magazine advertising lessened their effectiveness. For all practical purposes, pocket mirrors have gone the way of horsewhips as items of common manufacture. Mirrors made from photographs of important candidates can sometimes be seen today during national political campaigns *(Fig. 19)*.

Fig. 17

Portrait of Sir Winston Churchill; woven by Brough, Nicholson
& Hall, Ltd. in 1965.

Modern Silk-Woven Pictures

by J. R. GOFFIN

GENERALLY, WHEN silk-woven pictures are discussed, people think of the products from Thomas Stevens' factory at Coventry, England, where over a century ago he first started to weave the silk bookmarks and ribbon pictures known as Stevengraphs. Today these are widely collected and expensive.

Yet, it is possible to build up a collection of modern silk-woven pictures, woven on Jacquard looms in the style of Stevens, for very reasonable prices. Modern pictures are manufactured both in pure silk and in a rayon mixture so the word "silk" is used here in a generic sense to include both pure and man-made fibers. Besides comparing favorably with Stevengraphs, many modern silks have the additional advantage of being fadeproof. Only a comparatively small band of connoisseurs seem aware of their manufacture and, as the num-

bers woven are strictly limited, their appeal to the collector of modest means is obvious.

The intricacies of their manufacture are involved for the layman, but basically a Jacquard loom requires that cards be punched for each line in which each color is used. Many hundreds of cards are needed in the manufacture of even a very small picture. As an example, the British Christmas card produced by Textiles & Philately for Copecrest in 1971, (illustrated here), measures only 3 by 2 1/4 inches, yet 1,394 cards were required to weave its six weft colors.

Craftsmanship of a high order is necessary, for it is only by the subtle use of different weaves and careful intermingling of colors that variations of tone and shading—so vital if a picture is to spring to life—are achieved. The prep-

A silk-woven Christmas card made by J. & J. Cash Ltd. for distribution to their customers.

The Golden Spike Ceremony; one of the "Great Moment" Series produced by Textiles & Philately for Copecrest.

Gawsworth Old Rectory, Cheshire, England; a superb silk picture woven by Brocklehurst-Whiston in 1963.

aration of the design, the Jacquard cards and the weaving, are too time-consuming for woven pictures to be considered economical under modern conditions; today they are mainly produced to commemorate special events or for publicity and prestige purposes.

J. & J. Cash Ltd. of Coventry, England, known throughout the world for their woven and printed labels, ribbons, trimmings, and name tapes, are among the small number of firms who have manufactured modern silk-woven pictures. To mark the City of Coventry's 900th anniversary in 1967, they issued a simple black and white picture of the Coventry statue of Lady Godiva, measuring approximately $4^3/4$ by $2^1/4$ inches and neatly framed in white card. As a companion piece they made a silk bookmark in deep blue showing the same design woven in gold thread.

Lady Godiva; a simple black and white silk picture woven by J. & J. Cash in 1967 to commemorate the City of Coventry's 900th anniversary.

Among Cash silk pictures that can still be bought from the Cathedral Office at Coventry are an exterior view of the cathedral, St. Michael and the Devil, the Baptistery Window and Font, the "Tablets of the Word," and a splended reproduction of Graham Sutherland's huge tapestry which hangs behind the high altar of the cathedral. The original tapestry, the largest in the world, measures 75 by 40 feet. Cash has cleverly reduced this to a perfectly colored facsimile just $5^1/2$ by 3 inches, to make an ideal souvenir of the new cathedral. None of these pictures cost more than $1.

Cash also sends out to the trade and customers specially woven sample pictures as Christmas cards. These are attractive but unfortunately are not available to the general public and no silk pictures can be bought direct from Cash.

At the time of Queen Elizabeth II's coronation in 1953, Brough, Nicholson & Hall Ltd. of Leek, Staffordshire, England, produced two types of woven bookmarks in pure silk, one being for the British market, the other for the sale abroad. Each type showed a slightly different portrait of the Queen, but both possess the same parchment-colored background and gold-colored tassel. The same firm also manufactured a magnificent, pure silk, black and silver

Christmas design issued in 1971 by Textiles & Philately for Copecrest which harmonizes with the special stamps issued by the British Post Office at Christmas that year.

Sulgrave Manor, home of George Washington's ancestors;
Brocklehurst-Whiston silk picture woven in 1960.

portrait head of Sir Winston Churchill at the time of his death in 1965. Approximately 4 by 3 inches, this is a first-rate example of the weaver's craft and worthy of the firm who bought Thomas Stevens' old factory after the Second World War.

Also produced to commemorate the 1953 coronation and measuring some 5³/₄ by 3¹/₄ inches was a silk-woven colored picture of Queen Elizabeth II being crowned inside London's Westminster Abbey. This came from the Brocklehurst-Whiston Mills at Macclesfield, Cheshire, England. Between 1946 and 1969 this firm produced 17 different pictures in pure silk. Unfortunately no records were kept of the numbers manufactured, but it is estimated that about 3,500 copies of each design were woven. Made for presentation to customers at Christmas or the New Year, the majority show Cheshire scenes, but there is an interesting picture, woven in 1960, of Sulgrave Manor, Northamptonshire, England, the home of George Washington's ancestors.

The last picture woven by this firm, in 1969, depicts the sailing of the *Mayflower* from Plymouth in 1620. Designed by William Hine, the weavers were Marjorie Byrne and Marion Revill. Brocklehurst-Whiston pictures are larger than those from other manufacturers, some measuring as much as 7 by 4¹/₂ inches. Mounted in large, good quality folders which carry a printed description of each picture, they are among the most attractive.

Although not originally intended for sale to the public, examples of a few of

these pictures are still held by the firm and may be purchased by collectors. The collecting world is only just beginning to realize that Brocklehurst-Whiston pure silk pictures possess that special something which makes them particularly desirable. Over the last three years their price has steadily risen; examples of the few issues still available cost about $16.

At the time of the 1964 Stratford Festival, William Franklin & Sons Ltd.,

An "In Memoriam" picture woven in memory of General Douglas MacArthur by Textiles & Philately/Copecrest.

First Man on the Moon; a Textiles & Philately/Copecrest production.

formerly of Coventry and now at Banbridge, Northern Ireland, produced six pictures of Shakespearian characters. Each measured approximately 4 by 2½ inches. The set was uniformly mounted in gray card folders, the front leaves being cut out to represent the open curtains of a stage.

Another fine series of woven pictures is the result of an Anglo-American effort involving Textiles & Philately of England and Copecrest of Royal Oak, Michigan. Textiles & Philately arranges production in England while Copecrest distributes them in the United States. These Anglo-American productions are unusual in being of interest both to collectors of woven pictures and to philatelists who collect first day covers.

Since 1960 this Anglo-American team has issued a number of woven pictures to commemorate special occasions. These are mounted in specially printed cards bearing commemorative postage stamps cancelled with first day postmarks. For example, in 1969 a woven picture of Caernarvon Castle was produced to commemorate the Prince of Wales' Investiture there and the card bears the four special postage stamps issued at that time, complete with first day cancellations. A woven "In Memoriam" picture to General Douglas

MacArthur appears on another card with the special 1971 MacArthur stamp, while on the occasion of the first moon landing, a picture was woven showing the two astronauts erecting the Stars and Stripes on the moon's surface, the card bearing the special American moon stamp and moon landing postmark.

Also produced by Textiles & Philately for Copecrest is a new "Great Moment" series. These are woven pictures commemorating great moments in American history; they measure approximately 5 by 2¾ inches. Mounted in an attractive white card folder, each has printed notes describing in detail the event depicted. The four initial pictures in this series are "Lincoln's Gettysburg Address," "The Golden Spike Ceremony," "Battle of the Alamo," and "The Wright Brothers First Flight." Only 2,000 copies of each picture are woven and every card is numbered. It takes 45 minutes to weave each one.

Some of the later cards issued by this Anglo-American venture have the woven picture backed by a transparent cover. This leaves the reverse of the picture exposed, revealing the many colored threads used in the picture's manufacture so that the skill and craftsmanship involved in its production can be fully appreciated.

The History of Fishing

by EMMA STILES

Thick brown leather, plush lined case 14 x 10 x 9" contains trays of salmon flies, such as a single and double Jack Scott, Black Dose, Silver Doctor, Gypsy, Durham Ranger, Blue Doctor, Cock Robin, Causucpal, Ranger, Fairess Dark, Mitch, Butcher, Dusty Miller, Wilmots, Curtis.

Reels - Winds - Winches - Often referred to as "Side Winders" and "Knuckle Busters" by old time fishermen.

Photographs by the author of the Archie Stiles Fishing Tackle collection.

FISHING, FIRST for sport, later for food, has its beginnings in the most ancient of times. Slowly, through the ages, it has advanced from primitive man's sportive catching of fish in his bare hands to the intricate artistry of today's angler, measured by the way he handles his rod, casts his line, and the special techniques he uses in the operation of his reel.

In the dim ages, floods swept many lands. When the water receded, leaving fish stranded on beaches or in holes, the fisherman had only to make a snatch with his hands to catch a fish. In that age, before fish were known to be edible, such fishing was for fun only.

The second method was "tickling." When streams were almost dry and the only water of consequence was in pools, a fisherman leaning over a pool or stream needed only to slip his hand under the belly of the fish and tickle it. While the fish was enjoying such attention, the fisherman would open his fingers, spread them around the fish, make a sudden grab, and fish and water parted company. Fish fall easy victims to the "ticklers"; they will not dart away because there is nowhere to dart. Acquiring fish by "tickling" is still done in many countries. It is quite popular in the Rocky Mountain region of the United States, especially during droughts.

The third form of fishing, long before the Christian era, brought the spear into action.

The fourth method, originated by the Egyptians, was a crude form of modern line fishing. The Egyptians used a stout vine to which a burr was attached. When a small fish swallowed the burr, it was hauled in; a larger fish, which might disgorge the burr or break the vine, was pulled in as close to shore as possible and dispatched with a sharp blow of a club.

The Egyptians later devised a fishing line made of braided animal hair. They manufactured lines of unlimited length and attached them to thornwood branches which enabled them to cast well out from shore. The hair lines held the fish, but the burrs did not function satisfactorily with the big fish, so the Egyptians invented crude hooks made of bone, with one end sharpened. As time went on, people of other nations substituted ivory for bone, then bronze hooks, iron hooks, and steel hooks, The reverse barb on fishhooks is of modern creation.

About 3,000 B. C. the Persians started eating fish. The food value of fish was their secret for hundreds of years until the Assyrians learned about it. In time, fish became one of the principal food items of ancient nations.

About 900 B. C. the Chinese took up fishing. The Chinese were line fisherman at first, using braided silk, but since then have devised more ways of catching fish than any other nation.

India learned about fish as food about

Left: Wicker Creel. **Center:** Brass drying frame for drying linen line. **Right:** Trot (or Trawl) line to catch many fish; a stout line reaching across a stream, or for some distance along one bank, bearing at frequent intervals single hooks from short lines.

Rear row, left to right: (1) Pfueger Captain metal side winder. (2) Edward vom Hofe, New York, Pat. Sept. 2, 1879, famous dealer and manufacturer of fishing tackle. (3) Unidentified reel housed in a leather case. (4) Pfueger Everlaster. (5) Pflueger Ohio 1878. **Front row, left to right:** (1) Abbey & Imbrie, New York - solid brass reel; there is no breaking device to aid the angler with running fish. (2) Brigantine Ocean City Mfg. Co., Philadelphia, Pa. (3) Brigantine. (4) Free spool KingFisher Surf reel. (5) Pfueger Golden West 1878.

Hand-tooled leather First Aid Kit 5½ x 7½ x 4½". Blown glass bottles with glass stoppers carry prescription labels of "Savory & Moore, Chemists to the Queen, 143 New Bond Street, London."

Alcohol-burning stove and heavy tin soldered food containers housed in wicker basket. No manufacturer's name appears on these pieces.

Wicker picnic basket. No maker's mark on this set.

800 B. C. Their fishermen used lines, but depended chiefly on spears, with long stout vines attached to haul the spear back.

About 500 B. C. the Jews started fishing. They introduced the woven net, with which they were able to capture vast quantities of fish in a short time. This was the start of wholesale fishing and the beginning of a new enterprise.

The American Indians had several ways of fishing. One method was to use a hand line made of sinew or rawhide with a double-prong bone hook on which a piece of meat was placed for bait. A groove was worked in the bone, and little prongs or hooks worked onto each end. These bone pieces were not more than one inch long. Another method was a hand line made of rawhide, with a loop made of willow and a sharp prong of bone tied so the prong pointed up. When a fish swam into the loop, the Indian jerked up on the hand line, and the sharp prong would penetrate the fish. The loop would help to hold the prong in the fish so it could be taken from the water.

In shallow water the Indians used bows and arrows. They also used hand lances, spears, and traps. One of their fish traps was made of willow limbs the size of a finger, fashioned in the shape of a banana crate with a funnel-shaped end. Bait was placed in the traps which were sunk in deep water. The Indians took only enough fish to make one meal.

Historians agree that a crude reel existed in the 15th century and that the reel referred to as a "wind" was created about 1496 A. D. Barker's *The Art of Angling*, written in 1651, not only describes the reel and its use but also shows a drawing made in 1647 of a reel.

For centuries the idea existed that the early Egyptians had used a rod with a reel attached. This belief was created by Plaque 141 found in the tomb of King Pi which showed a man with a plain fish pole in one hand and with another pole in the other hand to which it appears a reel-like device was attached. Years later it was determined that while one pole undeniably was a fishing pole, the other, much stouter, had a knob on its end and undoubtedly was a club used to subdue the larger fish.

The first reels were called winds or winches. Isaak Walton, acclaimed as an author on the art of fishing, wrote of them as wheelers in 1653. Later the name was changed to reels.

Honest Isaak Walton, Patron Saint of Anglers, a tremendously popular and thorough sportsman, lives heroically in memory. Barker, referred to as "the father of salmon poaching," is practically forgotten. Barker's ambition was to catch many fish, ignoring laws, ethics, or another man's rights. Walton was the exact opposite. He was an angling missionary and made many conversions to the rod and reel.

Artificial fly fishing is unquestionably the most scientific mode of angling. It has not been established when the sport of fly casting originated, or where. Aelian, an Italian who lived from 170 to 230 A. D., is credited with being first to write on fly casting. His works are known as "Natural History Recordings." William Radcliff also declared that the book of *St. Albans,* regarded for centuries as the first volume on fishing printed in western Europe, was preceded much earlier by a book of 26 short chapters which was published in Antwerp.

Within 100 years of Isaak Walton's death, angling had gained so much popularity that fly casting contests were put on in various parts of England to determine the champion of each district. Real English sportsmen spurned every method other than casting to catch fish, and informal angling clubs resulted.

The first fishing club on the North American continent was organized in Philadelphia in 1732. Originally called

Left to right: Pocket-size heavy tin tackle box. Furnished line. Assorted wood and cork floats. Canvas air-fed floating minnow bucket. Salmon flies in folder. Fisherman's oil can. Bells attached to line tinkle when fish bite.

the "Schuylkill Fishing Company," it is now the oldest social club in the world. The organization still functions, now known as the "Fish House Club," with headquarters in Andalusia, Pennsylvania. It is probably the oldest sports body of any type in the matter of continuous existence. Annual meetings are held at which a toast is made to George Washington, who was an early-day guest; membership is limited to thirty.

Members of the American Rod and Reel Association, founded in the United States over a hundred years ago, pledged to fish only by casting. This organization lacked momentum until the formation of the Chicago Fly Casting Club in 1893 which, seizing upon the World's Fair as a medium of exploitation, staged the first United States national tournament. The events were: accuracy, accuracy fly, de-cay fly, long

Left to right: (1) Landing net with folding brass handle. (2) Ice Chopper, (3, 4 & 5) Fish Spears. (6) Gig. (7, 9 & 10) Rods put up in wooden forms. (8) Lancewood rod with extra tips. (11) Four section lap wind pole. (12) Salmon pole tip fits Butt No. 14. (13) Old wooden reel attached to rod.

distance bait, and long distance fly. The distances were 70, 80, and 85 feet. All casts were made on a lawn because methods for measuring casts on water had not been perfected.

Records of activities of the "Fly Casters" prior to 1861 are vague; however, there is a memorandum that a national tournament was arranged in 1861. It is believed that others followed periodically, but the 1893 event is the first which is replete with details.

The Chicago Fly Casting Club held the second national tournament in 1897, the third in 1903, and the fourth in 1905. At the fifth tournament at Kalamazoo, Michigan, in 1906, the idea developed into the National Association of Scientific Angling Clubs. The sixth tournament, held at Racine, Wisconsin, in 1907, was the first under the auspices of the A.S.A.C. This permanent organization was made up of the pioneer clubs: Chicago Fox River Valley, Grand Rapids, Kalamazoo, Kansas City, Racine, San Francisco, and Illinois. Recently other clubs have joined. The club is strictly amateur and governs the fly casting sport today. In January 1961, the name was changed from the "National Association of Angling and Casting Clubs" to "American Casting Association."

The fishing plug business started in America in the early 1900s. One of the first plug patents in America was issued to Jim Heddon, whose "Dowagiac Plug" is believed to be the first plug on the market. Among later vintage manufacturers were Bomber, Paw-Paw, Helin, Pflueger, and Wood. Most of the older plugs had wooden bodies and glass eyes. A few were made of light metal, parchment and bone. A prime collector's plug would be with body made of cork.

Antique Musical Instruments

French horn,
ca. 1900

by DR. JACK L. SCOTT

COLLECTING ANTIQUE musical wind and percussion instruments can be a fascinating hobby for people with an instrumental background—think of the millions of graduates of high school and college bands!—and for many non-musicians who find antique instruments decorative in their homes.

Though a baroque trumpet from the time of Bach may be difficult to find, the 19th and early 20th centuries provide many instruments for today's collector. The diversity of materials of which they were made—brass, copper, silver, rosewood, mahogany, and maple—adds to the interest of musicians and the zest of decorators.

From about 1840 amateur bands have provided a colorful facet of American life. By 1870 and up until 1910 nearly every town in the United States had its own band. In their colorful, sometimes gaudy, uniforms the local band was on hand to make parades, fairs, and holidays more festive, and band concerts in the town square were weekly summertime events.

Amateur bands reached their zenith between 1890 and 1910, when professional bands such as those led by Sousa were so immensely popular. Then, as victrolas, radio, and movies began to fill the entertainment requirements, amateur bands slowly but steadily lost their appeal. Trumpets and horns were packed away in their cases and carried to the attic to silently "grow antique" along with the bugles and flutes of ear-lier generations. The resurgence of school bands in recent years brought a demand for up-to-date instruments.

Finding antique musical instruments is usually by chance. Antiques dealers seldom keep wind instruments in stock although they may occasionally offer an instrument which has been acquired in an estate purchase. Once in a great while a real "oldie" may be found in a pawn shop. Long-established music companies often have old instruments which they have taken in trade in years past, saved for possible spare parts, and more or less forgotten; a good look through their repair shops may pay dividends. Probably the most rewarding source is the classified section of the local paper. A small ad evincing interest in old instruments frequently brings results.

Some of the instruments to be found, if you are constantly on the watch, are described below; those illustrated here are starred*.

The English bass horn* is one of the most curious of wind instruments from the 19th century and a grand prize for the collector. Made of brass, it served as the bass instrument for English and American military bands from about 1804 to 1840. The fingering mechanism consisted of open holes and keys; valves were not in common use until 1835.

Keyed bugle, ca. 1820

Cornet, ca. 1900

Coach horn, ca. 1840

English bass horn, ca. 1805

Flute, ca. 1830

Alto horn, ca. 1890

Similar to the English bass horn were the keyed bugles* which enjoyed great popularity from about 1815 to 1835. These bugles played the melody in bands prior to the invention of cornets and valved trumpets. They were usually made of copper, trimmed in brass, though many were entirely of brass. Their obvious obsolete feature is the keyed system similar to that of modern saxophones. Great numbers of them were manufactured and they may still be found today. The example pictured was found, unidentified, in an antiques shop in Mississippi.

The common military bugle with no keys or valves is also of interest to collectors and frequently available. Its important function in the 19th century was to give precise signals and directions to the soldiers in the field. The English bugles, of copper trimmed with brass, were rather short and fat with little flare to the bell. These date from about 1845 to the present day. The American bugles were larger with more flare to the bell; they were made of either brass or copper.

Picturesque is the word for the long slender coach horn* of the 19th century. Often measuring over 54 inches in length, it had tremendous carrying power and was played by coachmen on mail and passenger coaches to signal innkeepers of their approaching arrival. It also served notice to the passengers who could see but little from the windows of the coach that they were only moments away from a cheerful fire, warm food, and a long-awaited pint of ale for the gentlemen. In the latter part of the century gentlemen hunt parties carried coach horns, merely to add color to the hunt.

Coach horns from about 1840 to 1880 were made of copper and trimmed in brass. Later coach horns, 1880 to 1890, though still made of copper, were usually trimmed in nickel. Rare experimental horns, ca. 1895, were made of aluminum. In all the mouthpiece was soldered into the horn to prevent loss.

Reproductions of coach horns are on the market today but they are poorly made, and the imitation mouthpieces make them easy to recognize. Authentic coach horns have the same type mouth-pieces as do all standard brass instruments such as the cornet and trumpet.

The flute* for centuries has been the all time favorite instrument. Like all woodwinds, the earliest flutes were made of wood. Prior to 1800, flutes had few if any keys, and the various notes were produced by finger holes bored into the body of the instrument. Keys were gradually added, a few at a time, until the full key system as used today was developed in 1835. Wooden flutes were popular all through the 19th century and are still preferred in some European countries.

Metal flutes, usually of silver or silver-plated nickel silver, gained wide acceptance during the present century. The flute pictured is of rosewood and dates about 1830. Often found with a flute is its companion, the piccolo, about half as large.

Early clarinets are similar to early flutes in that they had far fewer keys than their modern counterparts. Although they were the same basic shape and design as modern clarinets, they were often made in light-colored wood whereas present-day clarinets are always dark-stained wood or plastic.

Drums are frequently forgotten in the consideration of antique musical instruments, but they can be colorful and in many instances linked with military history. Drums of the 19th and early 20th centuries had rope tension, that is, ropes were used to pull the two heads tight. Modern drums are tightened through the use of metal rods. Often military drums were highly decorated with military figures and mottoes. Drums of greatest interest to collectors are the parade drum which varies from 12 to 18 inches in height, and the large bass drum.

Functionally, a cornet*, trumpet, alto* or French horn* may be easily adapted to a lamp base, with one of the valves acting as light switch. Upright tubas have been used as umbrella stands, even as gigantic flower pots. Drums convert into storage bins for small toys or newspapers, or with tops added into coffee tables. Any of the old musical instruments, combined with pine or other greens, make into excellent Christmas arrangements.

Wine Labels

by CYRIL BRACEGIRDLE

WINE LABELS MAY not sound like exciting objects for the collector's interest, but as a medium of artistic expression they have in times past attracted the attention of such famous silver designers as Paul Storr, Matthew Boulton, and Hester Bateman.

These small utilitarian items also have the merit of great variety, including as they do almost 900 different designs, and being made in a wide range of materials—silver, Sheffield Plate, porcelain, mother-of-pearl, ivory, and enamels.

No one knows for certain when wine labels first began to be used, but it was probably about the middle of the 18th century when the aristocracy began to lay down cellars of port. Decanters made of cut glass were obviously unsuitable for any form of marking. The label or ring provided the answer.

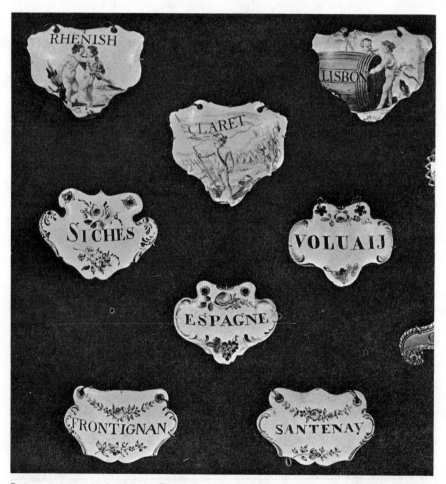

Battersea enamel wine labels. Those marked "Rhenish," "Lisbon," and "Claret," were painted by Ravenet; the others have black lettering on a white enamel ground, the flower and fruit ornaments in natural colors.

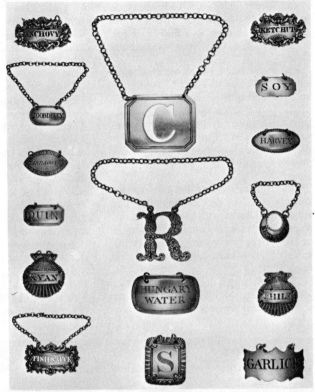

Except for the two initial-labels, a selection of condiment and food labels, all of silver.

In 1759 the Marking of Silver Plate Act was passed in England. Many of the Assay Offices, however, seem to have considered that wine labels were really not worth their attention. The many labels which escaped being marked during the first years of the Act have left a legacy of problems for today's collectors who may find labels marked only with the initials of the owner.

Silver was, in the beginning, the most popular material from which labels were made. Since labels were seldom engraved until a customer came along, the piercing of the descriptive material often obliterated part of the assay mark, rendering the collector's task of dating much more difficult.

From the 1760's Sheffield Plate, being considerably cheaper and equally decorative, closely rivalled sterling silver for labels in popularity. Here the collector should be warned that, all too often, what he thinks is Sheffield Plate will turn out to be electro-plated. Genuine Sheffield Plate items are scarce.

There were four distinct classes of wine labels: oblong, escutcheon, crescent, and oval. The oblong variety are narrow with a slight convexity, measuring about $1^{3/4}$ inches wide by $^{1/2}$ inch deep. The early examples are usually decorated with feathered edges, but by 1780, these edges were beginning to be bordered with a fine beading. A rarer type has double line borders or even a zigzag line.

In the early years, two holes would be bored just below the upper edges through which would run the ends of the chain, or perhaps a ring. Later, eyelets protruded from the edge. The slender chains and rings were invariably handmade in silver by female artists.

By 1807, an interesting type perforated with a letter, usually the initial of the owner, had appeared. Many of these were made for the use of individual customers in hotels or for members of exclusive gentlemen's clubs.

The escutcheon shape became fashionable in the early 1770s and continued until the end of the century. The edges of this type were mostly feathered, although in the early 19th century a variant appeared with fluted drapery on the sides. About 1830, the escutcheon was revived, edged now with elaborate mounts.

The crescent shape belongs to the same period as the oblong and has widespread horns with eyelets for chain rings. They can be found with double or even triple line borders. Some of the early 19th century examples have vine decoration.

The oval, edged with bright cutting, was in fashion by 1790. Its flat surface was made to fit against the sloping neck of a cut glass decanter. From 1825, some most attractive examples were made in the shape of a vine leaf, sometimes with a bunch of grapes included. The loop or bottle ring also dates from 1790.

In the brief period between 1753 and 1756, some beautiful labels were made in enamel at a factory in Battersea. These colorful copper objects, covered with white enamel, were decorated by transfer printing. Almost all of the Battersea labels were decorated by an artist named Ravenet, who used at least a score of different designs featuring cupids, satyrs, and fauns. A genuine Ravenet wine label is an expensive find today.

Enamels were also made in Staffordshire. These are more plentiful today and much less valuable than those made at Battersea but may easily be confused with them The Staffordshire products are usually escutcheon-shaped,

Five shield-shaped porcelain labels, black lettering with gold edges and vintage decorations. Oval "Champagne" label (center, bottom), white enamel on copper with green leafage decoration. Pierced rectangular "Port" and "Claret" labels of gilt beaded wire set with colored glass rectangles. The small "Eau de Rose" silver label (center, top) surmounted with a cherub's head was most likely made for a cologne bottle label.

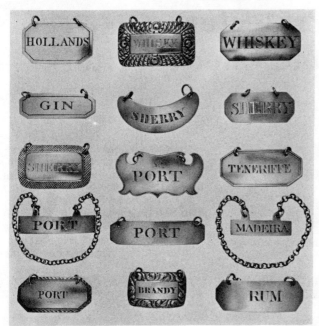

Silver wine and spirit labels in various shapes.

measuring about 2 by 1¹/² inches, and having the name of the wine in black lettering, with a floral spray design or perhaps a rose or a bunch of grapes in natural color.

It is sometimes possible to find examples of rare Eastern labels, even some of gold from India, or of tiger's claws or boar's tusks from Asia. However, beauty and variety of design remain the major aspects of wine labels which attract the collector.

Allied to wine labels are bin labels.

These are small discs of pottery about 3 inches in diameter. Some are glazed, some unglazed, and they bear a number which would be that of a ledger reference in the wine cellar. Bin labels were made by Wedgwood, Spode, Minton, Davenport, and of Delft.

In 1860 a law passed in England requiring all wine bottles to be marked with a paper label effectively finished the manufacture of wine labels. Few were made after that date.

Check Protectors
and Check Writers

by F. M. Gosling

Fig. 1

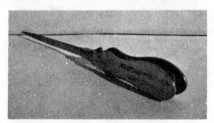

Fig. 2

as the check is pulled out, thus embossing the paper and making alteration difficult. This device bears a U.S. patent date of "Ja. 7, 1902."

Fig. 2 is a $7^1/^2$ inch long letter opener. Stamped on the handle is "Compliments of Martin H. Smith Co., New York, N.Y." The handle is in two parts, both of which have serrations on the

Fig. 3

FOR AS LONG AS checks have been used to transfer money, unscrupulous persons have used their wits to alter checks, raising the amounts and cashing them to their own benefit.

At least two methods have been developed to combat this practice. One has been the use of safety paper, made in light colors with a design on the surface which will come off it if it is tampered with.

The other method, which can be used in conjunction with the first, is the employment of mechanical devices known as check protectors or check writers. Many of these have become obsolete and can now make an interesting collection.

Several different types are shown here.

Fig. 1 is a piece of spring steel, $2^1/^2$ inches long, $^3/^4$ inch wide, with serrated rollers on the ends. The check is inserted, with the amount between the springs. The rollers are held together

inside. By laying the opener flat, inserting the check, then striking the flat side of the handle with the hand, the same results can be achieved as in *Fig. 1*. No patent date is given.

Fig. 3 is a check protector, 4 inches long, made of iron. It operates like a small stapler but instead of stapling, it embosses the paper. It bears no manufacturer's name nor patent date.

Fig. 4 is the Page Pocket Check Protector, made in San Francisco, Calif. Patent dates shown are Oct. 1, 1912 and Feb. 22, 1916. It is $2^3/^4$ inches in diameter. There are figures from 0 through 9 and a dollar sign. On the back of each figure is mounted a group of small pins forming the numeral. The check is placed in a groove behind the number. When the number is pressed down with the fingers, the pins perforate the paper. This is a slow process as only one number can be perforated into the paper at a time.

Fig. 5 is somewhat more advanced. It can be classed as a check writer as it contains an ink roller and prints an embossed inked number. This is done by squeezing the handles together, which also advances the check to the next position. The steel numbers are on a wheel and are brought into position by turning the knob on the side. The number selected is indicated in an an opening at the top of the machine. Besides the numbers 0 through 9 there are the symbols "Pay," "$," "and," and " ¢ " . The lever in front of the handle can be pulled back to insert or remove the check. The cap forward of the release lever can be removed to add ink. It bears the name of the manufacturer, Arnold, Inc., Flint, Mich., the patent number 1,201,235, and "Pat's Pending," but no date.

Fig. 6 overshadows most check writers in both size and weight. Manufactured by Todd Protectograph Company, Rochester, N.Y., it measures 16 inches

Fig. 4

in length and weighs more than 7 pounds. Numerous patent dates are shown from 1901 to Feb. 1919. All numbers are spelled out and include 1 through 19, and 20 through 90 by tens. These, together with the words "No Cents," "Thousand," and "Hundred," can be embossed and printed on the check in red ink while the symbols "Exactly," "Cents," "Dollars," and "Not Over" appear in black. The check is fed into the machine via the adjustable

pan at the right side when the lever on the left side is pulled completely back. This same lever, which has a pointer attached, is then slid forward to the number to be used. The crank on the right is then given one complete turn, printing the spelled-out number and advancing the check one space. This machine appears to have better safety features than the others shown here; however it still was a slow process to select and crank out each separate figure. The writing out of a large amount could take up as much as 7 inches in length which would tax the capacity of most present day checks.

Numerals on today's check writers are designed to make figures difficult to alter. Try making a six into an eight! Also today's machines can do the job more quickly. One type employs a method used in processing credit cards where levers are advanced to the amount wanted, the check inserted, and printed with one pull of a lever. Another uses a keyboard similar to a full keyboard adding machine and operates in the same way—the amount is set up by depressing the keys and pulling the lever.

The day seems close at hand when check writing will be handled automatically, passing from some sort of card in a machine to a computer to the bank to the customer's account. Then even today's check writers will be obsolete!

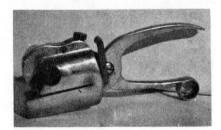

Fig. 5

Fig. 6

Bridle Rosettes

by CLARA NISBET

THE USE of bridle rosettes and other harness ornaments is steeped in folklore and history. Bits of shiny, flashing metal were long ago used on bridles as charms to protect horses from the Evil Spirits. A bronze figurine (338 B.C.) depicts an early form of rosette decorating the bridle of Bucephalus. Doubtless, it was of precious metal; only the best would have been good enough for the famous war horse which carried Alexander the Great through his campaigns.

Bridle rosettes, or bridle buttons, as they are sometimes called, are used in pairs, one on each end of the brow band where that strap slips over the crown piece. Those of pictured glass were usually made in a left and right version. Their position on the horse's head is an eye-catching one, an ideal spot for decoration. How well the manufacturers of rosettes met the challenge of their popularity is clearly seen in old harness catalogues where pages and pages of these ornaments are offered as "The latest thought in harness jewelry," or "To lend dignity and tone to any harness."

Of rosettes produced in this country, early specimens were of metal, followed in the 1850s by those of hard rubber composition. In the 1870s, the so-called "Picture Glass" rosettes appeared on the market.

These, with their almost unlimited possibilities of color and subject matter, met with immediate acclaim, and are prized by today's many collectors. Among subjects used were horses, people, dogs, cats, wild animals, emblems and designs, as well as sprays and bouquets of flowers. Initials were made in so many sizes and shapes, and in such variety of lettering and color combinations, that the collector can assemble a complete alphabet in which each and every letter is different in style. A few rosettes were made with colored glass — vaseline, amber, red, or blue.

The industry soared to a peak of popularity in the late 1800s and early 1900s, coming to an abrupt end with World War I. Mechanization spelled the doom of the great Horse Era, and forced many a commercial harness supply house to close its doors.

In the 1920s, a few firms resumed the manufacture of these ornaments. However, the new technique of mass production could not equal the quality of the carefully crafted originals. Many rosettes made in this later period show the use of brilliant, flashy colors or pictures of poor quality. Some were made with heavy, coarse loops, while in others the loop was omitted, readying them for conversion to lapel pins or brooches.

U. S. Military "brow band ornaments" can be accurately dated by their insignia. The rosette shown here has the asymmetrical eagle which was in use prior to 1834. It is 2 inches in diameter, of solid copper. We find great beauty of design in these early rosettes wrought of gold, silver, pewter, brass, tin, or copper. Combinations of these metals were also used effectively in designing monograms and crests.

Some metal rosettes are stamped with a maker's name: "Waldron," "Grilley," "Riker"; or with a date: "Pat. Sept. 6 R&Z 1886," "Pat. Sept. 13, 1888," "Pat. Mar. 11, '90," for examples. In her collection, Hilda Dineen reports a pair of silver dog heads dated 1872.

METAL ROSETTES

Of Hard Rubber

The oval rosette shown, 1¾ inches long, is of black, hard rubber composition. It is back-marked "I.R.C. CO. 1851 Goodyear." The engraved horse head, quite modern in feeling, originally had the design accented with gold or silver. W. H. Rosenberry has both the oval and the round versions of this rosette in his collection. A few undecorated rosettes in various shapes also have this back mark. Some of the later examples are marked "R&C.H.T.Co.," "N.S.Co.," or "F.T.Co."

Rosettes of this material were molded in varied shapes, either plain or with raised designs of simple a n i m a l   h e a d s , conventionalized flowers, geometric patterns or horsey emblems using whips, stirrups, spurs,

OF HARD RUBBER

horseshoes, and such. Some are found with the design of contrasting metal, making a striking effect.

Black was the color most often used, though some were made in white, yellow, tan, or red. The composition of these rosettes was brittle, making them too fragile for practical purposes; their manufacture was discontinued by the turn of the century.

"Pictured Glass"

The "Pictured Glass" rosette shown here is not only back-marked, "Pat. Nov. 16, '75," but also has the original label naming the horse on it as "Hopeful; Record 2:14¾." This gray gelding established his record in 1878, trotting on the Minneapolis track.

In rosettes of this type, the simple animal heads were inverted intaglio, hand-painted, on a 1-inch domed crystal. Though limited in scope, they represent a breakthrough in rosette manufacture, offering "Pic-

tured Glass" for the first time. The crystal is held securely in its metal mounting by a delicately etched, flat ¼-inch brass rim. There were later variations of the inverted intaglio type, some of which have "Pat. July 11, '82" stamped on the loop.

"PICTURED GLASS"

PAPER CUT-OUTS

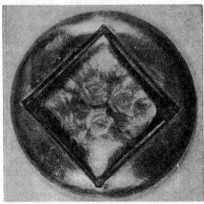

DECALCOMANIA

Paper Cut-Outs

The gay blade of the day might daringly sport, on the bridle of his high-stepper, a pair of rosettes portraying some lovely lady—an actress, even. The portrait shown of lady and cat is in shades of brown, enlivened by hand tinting—green for the dress, a dash of red for the comb. This rosette measures 1¾ inches in diameter, the convex glass being held in place by a rim of crimped brass.

Decalcomania

The early use of decalcomania, or transfer pictures, appears in the illustration of the novelty rosette with its attractive mounting of square, pictured glass set in a round, thick, brass rosette, 1¾ inches in diameter. The process of decalcomania opened a whole new field of color, of which rosette manufacturers were quick to take advantage. This rosette is backmarked "Mar. 14, 1882." Other rosettes of the more common glass-faced type bear this mark, as well as the date "Pat. Aug. 12, 1882," with some showing both dates.

"Pat. PP CO., Jul. 13, 09"

Rosettes, such as the one shown, 1¾ inches in diameter, with a 3/16-inch brass rim, as well as the dramatic 2½-inch version with ¼-inch brass rim, are stamped "Pat. PP CO., Jul. 13, 09." This is the mark of the Perforated Pad Co., Harness Accessories, of Woonsocket, Rhode Island. This company, after acquiring the Bryce Wilson Company, offered "rosettes in unlimited quantities" in their 1901 catalogue. Cards of rosettes, marked "Wilson Rosettes," were sold under the P.P.Co. name.

This is one of the few concerns still making rosettes, though today only the standard, glass-faced type is offered. The over-sized line, which included a 2-inch version of square, pictured glass in round brass rosette, has been discontinued.

Undated Rosettes

It is in the field of undated rosettes that the rosette industry hit its stride, offering literally hundreds of pictures in various shapes, sizes, and settings, some with rims having such patterns as rope, gadroon or

"Pat. PP CO., Jul. 13, 09"

UNDATED ROSETTES

fleur-de-lis. It is doubtful if any one collector has been fortunate enough to assemble them all, though some collections run into thousands.

From the group of wild animals, which is quite limited, the "rabbit" rosette pictured has a whimsical quality, and is so reminiscent of "Rabbit" in *Alice's Adventures in Wonderland* as to lead one to surmise it was created especially for the pony-cart set.

Mention should be made of an excellent group of rosettes, undated, but having the stamp "Pfluegers, Patent U. S. & Canada." These are the glass-faced type, with pictures of fine quality, and fine construction.